TERRACE HILL
The Story of a House
and the People Who Touched It

Scherrie Goettsch and Steve Weinberg

WALLACE-HOMESTEAD BOOK CO.
1912 GRAND AVENUE
DES MOINES, IOWA 50305

ISBN 0-87069-243-7
Library of Congress Catalog
Number 77-91487

PUBLISHED BY

WALLACE-HOMESTEAD BOOK CO.
1912 GRAND AVENUE
DES MOINES, IOWA 50305

Table of Contents

Preface

Terrace Hill, the best-known house in Iowa, has fascinated countless people. But nobody had published a thorough history of the mansion or its larger-than-life residents during the first 110 years of its existence. This book is an attempt to fill that gap. Its origins go back to 1971, when one of the authors moved into the mansion's basement as a live-in caretaker.

The book is not meant to be scholarly, although it is based on extensive research. It was not written primarily for an audience of professional historians. Footnotes, for example, are not included. However, a bibliography is at the back for readers interested in further exploration. We began by reading every history of Iowa that we could find. But we culled little of use from such general sources. And often, further checking showed that what we had learned was inaccurate. As a result, we relied on primary sources whenever possible. Those sources included land records, legal documents located in court archives, and personal interviews with persons who had firsthand knowledge about Terrace Hill and its occupants. We supplemented primary sources with information from newspapers dating back to 1850, and old photographs.

Assistance was received at every turn from people with an interest in Iowa history. It would be impossible to thank everyone by name, but we do want to express our special gratitude to several. Judy Gildner, editor of the *Annals of Iowa,* read the first draft of the manuscript and made suggestions that led to many revisions. Lida Greene, head librarian at the State Historical Museum and Archives in Des Moines, tracked down documents we never would have found on our own. State Treasurer Maurice Baringer and his secretary Ruth Van Note provided aid that made this book more complete than it otherwise would have been. Samuel Klingensmith, an architectural historian for the State Division of Historical Preservation in Iowa City, shared the knowledge of Terrace Hill he gained while conducting his own research. William Wagner, the Des Moines architect in charge of the restoration, answered questions from his storehouse of information, as did his associate Lawrence Ericsson. Mary Belle Windsor and Frances Ingham, both of Des Moines, searched their memories and their attics for tidbits about life in Terrace Hill when they were being reared there. Elmer Nelson, a former chauffeur for the Hubbell family, and Nelson's daughter Frances Tometich, communicated their reminiscences of the mansion from California. Paul Ashby, an amateur historian whose passion is lore about Des Moines, shared his collection of historic photographs with the authors. James Leonardo, a librarian at Drake University in Des Moines, helped guide us through the intricate maze of local and state history. Bob Knecht, an archivist at the Federal Archives and Records Center in Kansas City, Missouri, and his colleagues went beyond the call of duty to locate documents concerning Benjamin Franklin Allen, the builder and first inhabitant of Terrace Hill.

The tale of Terrace Hill is far from finished. The mansion is still changing. Now the home of Iowa's governor, it will probably inspire other histories in future decades. But it is our hope that this book is a thorough account, as of today, of the mansion and the people whose personalities have shaped it.

Scherrie Goettsch and Steve Weinberg
Summer 1978

5

Introduction

When Iowa Gov. Robert Ray and his family moved into Terrace Hill during 1976, their occupancy seemed fitting. Ray, serving an unprecedented fourth term as governor, was in many people's minds the most powerful man in Iowa. So it seemed only proper that the governor reside in the Victorian mansion that had been the home of two other men who in their day were also thought to be the most powerful in Iowa.

The first of those inhabitants was Benjamin Franklin Allen, who built Terrace Hill 110 years before it became a governor's residence. Allen had settled in Iowa in 1848 at age nineteen when today's capital was the settlement of Fort Des Moines. Iowa had been admitted to the Union just two years earlier. By the time the plans for Terrace Hill were unveiled in 1866, Fort Des Moines had dropped the first word from its name and was showing signs of becoming a bustling city. Allen had become a millionaire. Terrace Hill was his monument to his wealth. Allen spent at least $250,000 on the construction and furnishings. Translated into today's currency, that sum would make Terrace Hill a multimillion dollar home.

Unlike Governor Ray, Allen derived his power from his banking, landbuying, and numerous businesses, not from politics. When Allen's empire collapsed just seven years after Terrace Hill was completed, he took thousands of people with him as he was pushed into bankruptcy. For a decade, during which time disputes with creditors went all the way to the U.S. Supreme Court, the fate of Terrace Hill remained uncertain. The house fell into disuse. As it had been a symbol of Allen's power, so it became a symbol of his downfall.

The second of Terrace Hill's powerful inhabitants was Frederick Marion Hubbell, who bought the mansion from Allen in 1884. By then, Allen was in disgrace. Hubbell already had bought much of the valuable land in Des Moines since arriving from the East in 1855. He often made his purchases from down-and-out owners, and exercised the same shrewdness with Terrace Hill, paying just $60,000. Hubbell lived there for forty-six years, until 1930. He died there, in the mansion that was his own symbol of power. At his death, Hubbell was proclaimed the richest man in Iowa history. That probably remains true today.

Governor Ray's move into Terrace Hill was fitting not only because of his power, but also because the move occurred in the midst of great controversy over the mansion. It seemed as if the house had been controversial from the day plans for it were announced by Allen. The controversy at the time of the governor's occupancy in 1976 involved cost overruns. When the state of Iowa accepted the house as a gift from F.M. Hubbell's heirs in 1971, nobody was certain how it would be used. But with cost estimates for conversion into a governor's residence at a seemingly reasonable $250,000, the idea gained acceptance. However, by the time the governor's family moved in, work on Terrace Hill had cost more than $1 million, with the end nowhere in sight.

Critics said the mansion had become a drain on Iowa taxpayers. One was State Sen. Earl Willits. "They are going to have $3 million in it by the time they are done," Willits said. "We could have built a beautiful new mansion for $1 million. At the time I supported it, but in retrospect it was a mistake. We never got any accurate cost figures." The critics did not prevail, though. The house retained its fascination for people throughout the state. Citizens were clamoring to get inside the mansion. Security guards said they had to turn away would-be visitors regularly. One guard said he had heard every possible excuse: "They say things like we used to rake leaves here, or we used to know the Hubbells. Sometimes they'll even go so far as to say they're friends of the governor."

Controversy, as already noted, had engulfed Terrace Hill prior to the 1970s. In the days of Allen and Hubbell, the highly visible mansion was talked about constantly, not only throughout Iowa but also throughout the nation by people who had seen it or heard of it. Then as now, opinions were sharply divided. One admirer was the editor of the *Iowa State Register,* who said of the mansion when it passed from Allen to Hubbell in 1884: "It stands on one of the highest points of land around Des Moines, and overlooks as pretty scenery as can be found anywhere outside the grand scenery of a mountainous country. On this site Mr. Allen built a home which would have been a credit to any city, and he showed his great faith in Des Moines at that time to build. Many thousands of people from all parts of the country have visited the place, and admired its beauty." That praise came after Allen had fallen, and after the newness of the mansion had worn. Even more exuberant words were written when the home was first viewed by persons attending the 1869 housewarming, on the occasion of Benjamin and Arathusa Allen's fifteenth wedding anniversary. One newspaper account said: "For the old settlers to realize that their Des Moines was graced with the most magnificent private residence, and the most luxuriantly equipped, west of the far-off Hudson River was not possible without bewilderment. For a young town, away out here on the prairie sea, to eclipse good old Cincinnati, ambitious Chicago, and aristocratic Saint Louis, is no light honor to bedeck the capital city of Iowa with. Few

When this Franco-Italian villa was opened in 1870 by Jedidiah Wilcox, it was the most costly house ever built in Connecticut. Beechwood cost an estimated $200,000. (Courtesy Meriden Public Library, Tom Caneschi photograph.)

This Second Empire mode house was built as a summer home in the late 1860s. Maplewood, a fine example of post-Civil War architecture, was the only known Second Empire house in Fairfax County. This photograph shows evidence of the removal of much of the original ornamentation. (Courtesy County of Fairfax.)

men have $250,000 to spend in fitting themselves a home, and Des Moines is the only city in the West which has a gentleman who has done it.''

Other observers were unimpressed. Cyrenus Cole, a contemporary of Allen and Hubbell, thought Terrace Hill had no business being built, much less lauded. In his memoirs, Cole said: ''The ultrasocial center of Des Moines during the gay nineties was Terrace Hill, which stood on the top of Snobs' Hill. It was the home of Mr. and Mrs. Frederick M. Hubbell. A foolish man had built the big house and a wise man was then living in it. The foolish man was a Mr. Allen, who wanted to make Des Moines bigger than it was and also bigger than there

was any need of its being. . . . In due time Mr. Hubbell came along and picked up many of the things Mr. Allen had dropped by the way. . . . When he became the wealthiest man in Des Moines, Terrace Hill became its social center, although neither Mr. Hubbell nor Mrs. Hubbell ever seemed to care much about society—they merely entertained it. When men or women could say offhand that they had been invited to Terrace Hill, their social standing was secure. I think all this kind of pother must have made the master of the house smile.''

When that master died in 1930, the mansion faced an uncertain future. Most of Hubbell's heirs thought it was too expensive to care for, too impractical to be used as a family home. Hubbell's eldest son rejected living there. But Hubbell's youngest son, Grover, put family tradition ahead of practicality. Until his death in 1956, Grover Hubbell and his wife Anna presided over Terrace Hill. After Grover's death, however, the house threatened to become just a memory. Guardians of the nation's architectural treasures feared it would be torn down, something that was befalling Victorian mansions across the country. For example, Beechwood—the Jedidiah Wilcox house in Meriden, Connecticut—was demolished while the fate of Terrace Hill was in question. Beechwood, similar in appearance to Terrace Hill, had been built in the same year. Three of its rooms were preserved for display in the New York City Metropolitan Museum of Art, but that was not the same as having the mansion still standing. Maplewood, a mansion in Fairfax County, Virginia, whose appearance also was similar to Terrace Hill, was torn down about the same time as Beechwood. But that fate did not befall Terrace Hill. Terrace Hill was a Victorian classic when built, and remains so today. Its characteristics, such as the steeply pitched roof, open verandas, long and narrow paired windows, bracketed eaves, and jigsaw needlework, make it an irreplaceable design form. And although it was uninhabited except for caretakers for nearly two decades after Grover's death, its existence was finally assured when the state took possession. It has not been forgotten since then either, with supporters and detractors arguing over the mansion regularly.

The construction of Terrace Hill and its endurance through so many upheavals are integral parts of Iowa history. The mansion has contributed to the state's architectural, social, political, and economic fabric. But a book about Terrace Hill cannot be about bricks and mortar alone. Any house is built and altered by men and women. A history of Terrace Hill would make little sense without an understanding of the people who touched it, and whose lives it touched in turn. The history of the house is tied to Benjamin and Arathusa Allen, Frederick and Frances Hubbell, Grover and Anna Hubbell, Gov. Robert and Billie Ray, and others. This book intertwines the evolution of Iowa's best-known residence with the lives of people who, it so happened, had a major effect not only on Terrace Hill but also on the history of Iowa.

Chapter One

Allen's Ascendancy

When Benjamin Franklin Allen arrived in Fort Des Moines, building a mansion like Terrace Hill was not in his thoughts. Allen arrived at the sparsely settled outpost in 1848 as an orphan nineteen years of age. His parents had died within a week of one another when Benjamin was four. His father, a respected printer-publisher, and his mother were stricken by cholera in their hometown of Salem, Indiana. An account of their deaths said that Benjamin was left "with nothing but poverty for a heritage." The boy did not become a hard-luck case, however. He was sent to his grandfather in Brown County, Ohio, where he remained until old enough to earn money on his own. Allen then returned to Indiana, where he apparently worked on a farm during the summers and attended school during the winters. Although documented information of Allen's boyhood is sparse, Nettie Sanford, a central Iowa pioneer and journalist, wrote inspirationally of the youthful Benjamin in Indiana as he made his first dollars "selling peaches and other fruits." Sanford called Benjamin's early years "an example worthy of imitation by the young men of the country."

In 1846, seventeen-year-old Allen entered military service at New Albany, Indiana. He served as a wagonmaster under the protective eye of an uncle, Robert Allen, who was a quartermaster in the U.S. Army. Benjamin remained in service about two years during the Mexican War. After being discharged at New Orleans, he made his way to Fort Des Moines via Franklin, Indiana. Despite later stories of Allen's poverty-stricken youth, his arrival at the Iowa settlement was not the beginning of a rags-to-riches saga. Allen in fact was a well-to-do adolescent when he arrived. His property came from a benefactor, Capt. James Allen, Benjamin's bachelor uncle. In 1843, the captain—a West Point graduate and career military man—established an Army outpost at the confluence of the Des Moines and Raccoon rivers, near today's downtown Des Moines. His assignment was to protect the Sac and Fox Indians from white squatters trying to claim lands belonging to the tribes. While Captain Allen was at Fort Des Moines, he looked out for his own interests at least as well as those of the Indians. His business ventures included opening the first coal shafts and the first stone quarry in Polk County, on the banks of the Des Moines River. He also founded a lumber sawmill, later adding facilities for grinding wheat. By the time Captain Allen re-

ceived orders to abandon Fort Des Moines in 1846, he had built profitable businesses, ones to which he may have intended to return. But he never got the chance. With the outbreak of the Mexican War, the captain was ordered to recruit Mormons living in the Midwest and march them into Mexico. On the march, the captain took ill. He died August 23, 1846.

Exactly where Benjamin Allen was at the time of his uncle's death is uncertain, but it is certain that Benjamin had listened in years past as his uncle spoke glowingly of Fort Des Moines. So, Benjamin decided to make the Iowa settlement his base of opportunity. How much money he brought with him is not known for sure, although there were rumors the sum was great. One historian wrote that the youth arrived carrying "about fifteen thousand dollars, in those days deemed a large sum." Another chronicler of Polk County history said that Allen arrived "with considerable cash capital." Whatever amount Allen brought to Fort Des Moines, it was supplemented by Captain Allen's property already there.

Some people were suspicious of so much money in the hands of a youth. Stories circulated that the money was ill-gotten during the Mexican War. As one newspaper article later told it: "The Mexican War spawned the Iowa banker (Allen), then in a sort of tadpole phase, and with him there were also about 5,000 pillar dollars which once used to hide their shining faces in the Halls of the Montezumas." The bulk of Fort Des Moines' early settlers, however, were almost surely pleased to have Allen arrive in town with his money, whatever its sources. The town needed capital desperately: Allen helped fill that need. With partner Jonathan Lyon, Allen opened a general store at Second and Vine streets. Thanks to his uncle the captain, Allen stepped into other ventures as a part-owner. There was the three-story water mill on the river, a multi-purpose facility that ground corn into meal, milled wheat into flour, and sawed logs into boards of lumber. There was also the kiln located by the clay beds north of town, where workers produced bricks for fireplaces and chimneys.

Allen had not been in Fort Des Moines long when he and his friend Charley Van decided to establish a steam sawmill near the south end of the Raccoon River bridge. The venture was popular, because the citizenry needed lumber for building houses and commercial structures. Lumber was being hauled in from afar, often over nearly impassable trails. With black walnut trees growing in abundance by the river, why not make use of the resources at hand, Allen reasoned. The town's newspaper, the *Iowa Star,* was excited over the future of the settlement because of the Allen-Van sawmill and another under construction by men named Dean and Cole. The newspaper said in early 1850: "Then will be heard on either side of the river the shrill whistle of the panting engine, while our streets will resound with the noise of the hammer and the saw, and broad and deep will be laid the foundation of many a stately edifice. Our town will emerge from infancy to youth, from youth to a vigorous manhood, and its area will be extended over the beautiful slopes that surround it.''

Despite Allen's ambitiousness, Terrace Hill, of course, was not even a gleam in his eye in 1850. He did not yet own the land on which the mansion would sit, a site at that time considered to be far out in the country. But the newspaper's prediction of how the town would have ''stately edifices'' would come true in a way that the editor did not then imagine. Allen, meanwhile, was living in a rented room at the Marvin House, Third and Walnut streets, rather than in a mansion. It could not have been known at that time, but he and other renters there were to play major roles in the growth of Des Moines. The names included Hoyt Sherman, Billy Moore, Andrew Jackson Stevens, and Madison Young.

Allen kept testing new fields to increase his fortune. In 1849, he was named as a delegate to an eight-county convention to promote railroad building. It would be seventeen years before Des Moines would get railroad service, but Allen saw the need for it from the start. Another venture was begun in 1851, when Allen and a partner bought a steamboat to carry goods to Fort Des Moines from points south. Within three years, the Fort Des Moines Steamboat Co. was formed, with Allen as a leading stockholder. The company ran boats on the Mississippi and Des Moines rivers. It also constructed docks, warehouses, and storerooms.

Allen did not ignore his general store, either, although his efforts at expansion were not always smooth. An impetuous, gambling businessman in later years, Allen gave a hint of those traits as early as 1849 when he traveled to Ohio to buy goods for the store. Although cautioned by his partner not to buy more than $35,000 worth, Allen went far beyond that amount. After visiting Cincinnati, he continued to Philadelphia and New York City, purchasing merchandise worth about $110,000. The freight bills alone were $6,500. For weeks, the merchandise continued to arrive at Fort Des Moines, filling every nook in the store plus all the barns the firm could rent. Historian Johnson Brigham, told of the incident by Allen's clerk Billy Moore, wrote that Allen's partner Lyon was ''appalled. He swore he was a ruined man, and that bankruptcy was inevitable unless something could be done to work off the goods.'' One thing that was done was to send Moore and six wagonloads of goods to the Warren County town of Summerset, near present-day Indianola, where there was no store to match Allen's. Moore sold the merchandise in no time.

Allen was clearly a promoter. An 1850 newspaper advertisement for his store was flamboyant, giving an indication of Allen's facility at making money that eventually allowed him to build a residence like Terrace Hill. To let the public know that the store carried everything from ''a silk dress to a goose yoke,'' the advertisement contained a poem of six stanzas, three of which read:

We've everything to please the eye,
Upon this distant shore;
And goods enough to fill the sky,
And just a little more. . . .

We've prints and screws and threads and fish,
All from the Atlantic shore,
And everything that man can wish,
And just a trifle more!

By wind and tide our bark was tost
Upon the Des Moines shore.
We mean to sell our goods at cost,
And just a trifle more.

The advertisement also attempted to cajole customers into paying their bills in a more timely fashion, noting that ''unlike that wonderful animal the chameleon, we cannot live on air.'' Allen and Lyon said that in payment for debts and goods, they would accept ''all kinds of country produce,'' including corn and wheat delivered to Parmalee's Mill in their name.

With that kind of cleverness at work, combined with a high demand for goods in short supply on the frontier, it was no wonder that Allen ran a successful store. Sometimes it must have seemed to townsfolk that whatever young Allen touched turned to riches. In the late 1840s, he began buying land from the state of Iowa that had been dispensed by the federal government. Allen later recounted his decision to become a land purchaser on a large scale: ''When I first went to Iowa in the fall of 1848, the land then belonged to the government, not subject to entry at that time. I bought squatters' claims. In that winter, after moving to Des Moines, the land in the region around Des Moines became subject to private entry and I entered considerable land with land warrants, and dealt in land from that time on. It was my principal business for some years.'' A study by historian Robert Swierenga of thirty-three counties in central Iowa showed Allen to be one of the top speculators in federally granted land. For example, in 1853, when he was still just twenty-four years old, Allen bought 1,560 acres in Madison County at an average price of $1.25 an acre. County courthouse records also indicated purchases of 2,880 acres in Boone County and 1,640 acres in Carroll County, among others. The study concluded that Allen bought 35,308 acres of government land in the thirty-three counties alone. He may have had thousands more acres in Iowa's other sixty-six counties.

Allen had much company—land speculation often was the road to overnight wealth in those days. Nonetheless, he stood out because of the quantity of his purchases. Allen had a vision that land would someday be in great demand, as Iowa was no longer regarded as the unsettled frontier. He foresaw railroad tracks laid on the land he was buying. Arden Holcomb, an early settler near Boone, wrote that in 1857 Allen bought

Mr. and Mrs. Francis R. West, parents of Arathusa Allen. (Courtesy Paul K. Ashby.)

Trees surround B. F. Allen's brick home built in 1856. The Allens lived here until they moved to Terrace Hill in 1868. (Courtesy Paul K. Ashby.)

636 acres at $13 an acre in expectation of the railroad coming through. In early 1859, Allen bought a 120-acre tract in Story County for a total of $210. It appears he expected a north-and-south railroad line to run through there in the future.

The Des Moines area was not ignored, either. For instance, in 1855 Granville Holland sold about thirty-four acres to Allen and Allen's father-in-law Francis West. That acreage was chosen by Allen as part of the site of Terrace Hill more than a decade later. In a separate transaction in 1855, Allen bought 331 acres for $500 from his father-in-law. From 1848, when Polk County land transactions were first recorded in permanent volumes, until 1875 when Allen went bankrupt, he was involved in a minimum of 1,100 property purchases and sales in Polk County alone.

While he was becoming a big-time wheeler and dealer, Allen was also establishing himself socially in the community. In 1850, he became a charter member of the International Order of Odd Fellows lodge in Fort Des Moines. In 1853, Allen was named a director of the Polk County Agricultural Society, which staged the first major farm fair in the county. But his most significant social advancement came when he married in 1854. Perhaps Allen did not have his social status in mind, but if Allen had chosen his wife with the idea of building bridges for the future, he could not have chosen better than Arathusa West, the daughter of a respected Fort Des Moines pioneer. The marriage was termed the ''greatest event in the social life of the year'' by journalist Nettie Sanford. Her account of the ceremony said: ''A splendid wedding held at Captain West's became food for gossip through many days. The bride was dressed in a silver gray silk, trimmed with soft white lace. White wax beads that looked like pearls were entwined with the braids of her dark brown hair, and at her nuptials she looked as charming as she does now in her diamonds and point lace.'' At the supper following the ceremony, there was music from a piano in the corner of the parlor—the first piano owned by anyone in Fort Des Moines, according to Sanford. The newlyweds did not go on a honeymoon, remaining instead in the home of the Wests for a few months while they organized their new life.

Within fifteen years, Benjamin and Arathusa would be the master and mistress of the grandest house in Iowa, perhaps in the entire Middle West. In the interim they did not do so badly, either. By 1857 they were living in a new two-story brick house at Fourth Street and Court Avenue. One observer termed it ''the marvel of the community.'' The house was noted for the parties given in it by the Allens. The Allens would occupy the house, along with their children, until the move to Terrace Hill, so Benjamin spared little in making it comfortable. Several years after it was built Des Moines Horticultural Society members toured the grounds, which were lush with dwarf fruit trees and ornamental shrubbery. The horticultural society reported that ''the commendable zeal of Mr. Allen has made this place an enviable spot. B.F. Allen's money, without B.F. Allen's personal care, labor, and watchfulness would have been a fruitless investment.''

The biggest plunge Allen took in those early years, however, was neither marriage nor the construction of a brick home. Rather, it was his entrance into banking. The business then was nothing like it is today. There were no layers of state and federal regulatory rules to safeguard the savings of depositors. That Allen was so successful so quickly in the cutthroat banking business was a tribute to his intelligence, his ruthlessness, or both. It was as a banker that Allen obtained the money to establish the fortune which allowed him to build Terrace Hill. And, although no one knew it in 1854 when Allen entered the business, it was to be through his bank dealings that Allen would suffer his downfall.

To understand how Allen operated as a banker, it is helpful to know about Iowa banking in the 1850s. When Iowa became a state in 1846, it prohibited banks from issuing money. But, according to banking historian Erling Erickson, the prohibition did not stop Iowa citizens from desiring an elastic currency. To meet the demand, substitute financial institutions were formed. Quite often, the entrepreneurs were called ''land agent bankers,'' who provided the services generally found at banks. Some of the land agent bankers, despite the state constitution, became issuers of money by circumventing the law. That was true of Allen's private bank, located on Second Street between Vine and Market streets.

A banking directory published in 1855 showed seven private banks in Fort Des Moines, including Allen's. There were thirty-eight banks in seventeen other Iowa towns. Little capital was needed to start a bank, making for easy entry into the field by operators who were not always scrupulous. Most private banks were small firms that did not physically resemble modern banks. Banking conditions were hectic, to say the least. Because Iowa-based banks could not legally issue money, the state became the dumping ground for wildcat notes issued by anybody who could get them printed. Des Moines historian L.F. Andrews described it like this: ''The country was flooded with notes of speculative, irresponsible banks. Merchants and businessmen would meet daily and prepare a list of banks deemed good for the day, at par, at discount, and worthless. The list would be revised on the arrival of each mail. . . . The conditions were ripe for counterfeiters and sharpers, and they got in their work, thus adding to the trouble. A merchant of this city went to Saint Louis to buy goods. He carefully selected the best notes he could find to pay his bills, but when he got there he could not get a dollar for the whole of them.''

Iowa's private bankers took advantage of the chaos by gaining control of banks outside the state and then circulating notes through their Iowa offices. Allen, not surprisingly, was in the lead. He secured a charter in 1856 from the Nebraska territorial legislature. The charter was advantageous to Allen, though not necessarily to the public. But Allen apparently practiced banking more honestly—at least early in his career—than did most of his competitors. When the financial panic of 1857 struck, Allen rode it out longer than anyone in Iowa. As late as April 1858, Bank of Nebraska notes were current. But the bank eventually did succumb. One report said that when the bank closed, its only assets were ''thirteen sacks of flour, one iron safe, a counter desk, stove drum, three armchairs, and a map of Douglas County (Nebraska).'' However, Allen did not pick up and run. He borrowed funds in the East to redeem outstanding notes. Few if any Bank of Nebraska billholders lost money. Despite the failure of his bank, Allen's reputation was enhanced. One newspaper account said later that during the crash of 1857, Allen the banker carried Des Moines' businessmen, saving some from going under. Even then, however, negative tendencies were noticed by a few who knew Allen. Stephen White, an early Fort Des Moines settler who later did business with Allen as a New York City stockbroker, said after Allen's downfall, ''He was inclined to dissipate money too much for a safe banker, I thought (in the early days). He would lend money too readily, and was too ready to take money at a large rate of interest with the hope of lending it at a larger. And having got money on hand which was payable on demand, he used it exactly as if it was his own.''

In 1857, Allen moved his private Des Moines bank from Second Street to the business block at Fourth Street and Court Avenue built by his father-in-law. The bank attracted visitors who marvelled at the fireproof vault complete with burglar alarm. The move to the new quarters coincided with the adoption in Iowa of a new constitution that legalized banks of issue. As a result, Iowa had its first locally issued currency since territorial days. Some influential persons, Allen among them, banded together to form the State Bank of Iowa. It was not actually a single bank, but rather a federation of independent banks. There were eventually fifteen branches approved, with the Des Moines branch one of the first on October 6, 1858. Allen, the largest stockholder, became president. Many persons who banked with Allen liked him because of his agreeableness to lending money on easy terms. It may have been that this stemmed from generosity, but it is more likely Allen was agreeable only after he was sure it would pay him to be that way. Records indicated that Allen the banker and Allen the land baron had dealings with just about everybody who was anybody in Des Moines. Well-known residents such as Hoyt Sherman who were to play vital roles in Allen's life after his downfall became indebted to him. Their dependence on his money—and his apparently fair treatment of borrowers—stood Allen in good stead. The high public opinion of Allen was one reason Terrace Hill was more admired than resented, despite its ostentation. And positive public opinion in those early days may have accounted for why Allen had staunch defenders in later years when he faced a prison term if convicted of fraud charges in his bank dealings.

Frank Mills, who operated a Des Moines printing business, was one person benefitting from Allen the understanding banker. Mills was able to expand his business with loans from Allen. "We owed him at one time through his three banks here (in Des Moines) and his two outside ones over $150,000," Mills said. "Bad banking it would be called now, but we were depositing much of the time near $1,000 a day. He had no other security than his faith in us, yet when he afterwards failed and final settlement was made there was a balance in our favor." Another example of Allen's early business transactions was recounted by the biographer of Edwin Ruthven Clapp, a Fort Des Moines pioneer. The recreated conversation between Clapp and Allen took place on a street corner around 1860. Clapp considered Allen to be a good friend, and as the conversation showed, Clapp got the loan he was seeking. But the conversation also showed that Allen asked some shrewd questions and did not say yes immediately.

Many people saw Allen not only as an agreeable lender but also as a man unselfish with his money. In the late 1850s, the Lutheran Church was having trouble raising enough money to finish building a college in Des Moines. (The town dropped the word "Fort" from its name in 1857, the same year it received a charter from the state legislature.) The Baptist Church eventually took over the project and completed it, but had nothing left for operating expenses. A Baptist fundraiser, without any appointment, dropped by Allen's private bank to ask for a contribution. He walked out with a $1,250 check from Allen.

Another example: During the Civil War, in which he did not fight, Allen contributed money to the families of men who agreed to enlist in response to a government plea for more volunteers from Iowa. Allen's $100 pledge was apparently the largest from any Des Moines businessman. Arathusa Allen helped, too, offering to work in town in place of men who went to the battlefields. Two days after Benjamin pledged his money, Arathusa affixed her name to a card that read: "We, the undersigned ladies of Des Moines, in view of the terrific conflict raging for the salvation of our beloved country, and the earnest call for troops raised by our patriotic executive, offer to take the places in business, as far as we are capable, of all patriotic men who will enlist and hasten to the support of our glorious husbands, sons, and brothers-in-arms. Brothers, to the rescue!" Allen was active in the Iowa Soldiers Orphans Home Association, which ran homes in Davenport, Cedar Falls, and Glenwood. In 1866, records indicated that Allen was treasurer of the group and also contributed $5,834.

Allen's fortune was sometimes tapped by poets, as well as by orphans. In the early 1860s, Leonard Brown published a book entitled *Poems of the Prairies* thanks to money from Allen. Brown, Polk County's schools superintendent, dedicated the volume to Benjamin and Arathusa. Benjamin was termed "that benevolent and public-spirited man of wealth. . . . Indeed,

no enterprise is undertaken for the public good in Iowa but he is a worker in it and contributes largely to it." Brown even wrote a poem to Allen, which read in part: "Allen, with gratitude I speak thy name/For I have had thy kindly help in need;/ Thou hast a loyal faith in God and man;/Jehovah's name thou honorest; and to thee/Is first of all God's works—Humanity." Having poems dedicated to him, however, did not cause Allen to abandon the profit motive. When Brown wanted to publish a non-verse book called *American Patriotism* several years later, Allen was skeptical about its chances. As a result, Allen advanced Brown $1,500, but insisted on Brown's home as security. The book did not sell well, and only by scraping together everything he could to repay Allen did Brown retain his residence.

In the 1860s, Allen became involved in a sphere other than economic. He ran for political office. He was elected to the Des Moines City Council from the Second Ward in 1860. He also became a mainstay in the Iowa Republican Party. One historian called Allen a member of the "Des Moines Regency," a faction that controlled the Republican Party for forty years. Like most Regency members, Allen was well-to-do. At age thirty-one he had accumulated $130,000 in real estate and $83,000 in personal property, according to the 1860 U.S. Census.

But politics remained a sidelight for Allen. He continued to concentrate his energy on building his financial empire. For example:

• He retained his private banking business, and in 1863 was named president when the State Bank of Iowa's Des Moines branch became a national bank.

• Allen continued to buy land throughout the state. But instead of buying only government land, he started attending sales where delinquent tax properties were on the block. The courts had traditionally held titles to land gained at tax auctions to be invalid; Allen, however, was having none of that. In 1864, in the case *Allen v. Armstrong,* the Iowa Supreme Court upheld several of his tax titles. He was thus encouraged to buy many more.

• His interest in railroads as strong as ever, Allen pledged $10,000 in March 1865 to encourage the Des Moines Valley Railroad to hurry its extension to the capital city, which was still without train service. Allen helped to raise an additional $90,000, and later that year traveled to Keokuk to tell the railroad's officers that their stock subscription goal had been reached.

• Also as the Civil War ended, Allen helped organize the first gas company in Des Moines. It was an important venture, because until then the means of illumination were tallow and lard oil. The gasworks was built at Second and Elm streets. The company—integrally tied to Allen—was successful financially until his collapse a decade later.

• Allen was an organizer of the Hawkeye Insurance Co. and became its treasurer. When formed in 1865, Hawkeye was the first property insurance company based in Iowa. Two years later, Allen would be deeply involved in the formation of the Equitable Life Insurance Co. of Iowa, the state's initial life insurer.

• When Wesley Redhead decided to move deeply into coal mining, he found Allen a willing backer. Mining had been in the Allen family: Discovery of coal in Polk County was credited to soldiers stationed at Fort Des Moines in the early 1840s, and Benjamin's uncle Capt. James Allen opened one of the first coal shafts. The mining industry did not take off, however, because wood for fuel was so plentiful. It was not until Redhead began mining systematically in 1865 around Des Moines that production grew substantially. In 1856, Polk County had produced just 600 tons of coal. A decade later the figure was 13,310 tons. By 1884, the year Allen sold Terrace Hill, the total was 619,921 tons. There was even coal found at the south end of the Terrace Hill property, along the railroad tracks.

• In the mid-1860s, Allen became more deeply involved in banking than ever before by obtaining controlling interest in the infant First National Bank of Des Moines from J.B. Stewart. The Second National Bank, another fledgling institution, was also purchased by Allen. He entered banking outside of the capital city by becoming president of banks in Atlantic and Indianola. And his railroading ventures were growing, too. They would soon contribute significantly to his fortune.

So, shortly after the Civil War, Allen dominated listings in Des Moines business directories. It seemed as if he were a part of every moneymaking venture in central Iowa. Later, there were dark hints that money for his transactions had come from illegal machinations with military funds during the Civil War. It was true that Allen's uncle, Robert, was an influential U.S. Army quartermaster during the war. But it remained unproven that Allen and his uncle had conspired, despite publication of charges in the *Chicago Tribune,* among other places. A hostile 1875 *Tribune* article said: "Allen sprang up in the night of civil war, thanks to a profuse watering and manurage at the hands of an uncle, who honored and improved the vocation of an Army quartermaster....The very troubles of (Benjamin's) country brought more grist to the Iowa mill—per favor, very largely of an avuncular quartermaster, who had it in his power to cash such vouchers as he pleased, and whose judicious selection of Mr. Allen's claims sped that thrifty person on his road to prosperity."

Chapter Two

The Most Elegant Residence in the West

Terrace Hill architect William W. Boyington. (Courtesy Chicago Historical Society.)

Whatever the sources of his wealth, legal or illegal, by 1866 Allen had acquired sufficient money to begin planning Terrace Hill. Allen certainly did not need to build such a mansion: The home at Fourth Street and Court Avenue was still magnificent by almost anybody's standards. It was also spacious enough for a large family. By late 1866, Arathusa and Benjamin had three children—Kitty, born in 1855; Benjamin, Jr., born in 1864; and Bessie, born in 1866. Harry would be born three years later. Two daughters, Fannie and Thusie, already had died in infancy.

What may have been the first public notice of the Terrace Hill project was published in the *Daily State Register* on October 13, 1866. It said Allen had hired workers several months earlier to prepare the grounds. The twenty-nine acre enclosure was situated on the summit of bluffs in what was then the far western part of Des Moines, between the Raccoon River and the Adel Road (today called Grand Avenue). When clearing of the site began, it was covered with a dense growth of hazel brush, scrub oak, and heavy timber. Some of that forest was retained for shade; most was removed. The work was done under the supervision of J.T. Elletson, a landscape gardener termed "skillful and tasteful" by the *Register*. The grounds would have grass-plats, flower banks, vineyards, and orchards, as well as graveled walks and drives throughout. At the highest point of land would be a water reservoir. It would be supplied from the Raccoon River, with water forced to the summit by a self-regulating windmill. The water would then be distributed to lakes and fountains on the grounds.

The *Register* said that all Des Moines was proud of what Allen was planning to do. The article called the site "the most attractive of any in the state," with a view of nearly every portion of the city. As for the house itself—to be started in 1867—it would be "one of the most elegant residences in the West. It will be not only an ornament, but a substantial improvement to the city. We trust its owner, who has accumulated his generous fortune by his own indomitable industry and business ability among us, will be spared to a ripe old age to enjoy the blessings of the home he is establishing," the *Register* said. Allen was not sparing any expense. Elletson had been brought in from New York state to do the landscaping. An 1862 advertisement by Elletson in a gardening publication said he was born in England, where he had worked at Buckingham Palace and Roby Castle. Elletson had been working around Geneva, New York, for about a decade before Allen's call.

The architect of Terrace Hill was also an out-of-state craftsman—William W. Boyington of Chicago. Born in Springfield, Massachusetts, Boyington studied architecture in New York under a top-notch professor. He moved to Chicago in 1853, and soon received his first commission—the old Central Union Depot. From then on, until the disastrous Chicago fire in 1871, Boyington designed not only other railroad depots, but also churches and secular buildings for numerous uses. Examples included the University of Chicago's observatory,

15

The Old Chicago Water Tower designed by W. W. Boyington, as it looked in 1869. The fanciful Gothic landmark is one of perhaps only four buildings of any kind to escape the great Chicago fire of 1871. (Courtesy Chicago Historical Society.)

Detail of drawing room fireplace mantle.
(Drawing by S. Goettsch.)

Crosby's Opera House, the Board of Trade Building, the Democratic National Convention Hall, the auditorium of the Grant Park Exposition Building, and numerous hotels, including the Sherman House, Farwell House, and Grand Pacific. His best-known prefire structure—mainly because it was one of the few buildings in the city to be unscarred in the ensuing conflagration—was the Old Chicago Water Tower, erected from 1867 to 1869, the same years as Terrace Hill. The water tower elicited plenty of comment. The playwright Oscar Wilde described it as "a castellated monstrosity with pepper boxes stuck all over it." The director of the Chicago Historical Society called it "quaint, even whimsical." There was little agreement on the body of Boyington's work, either. One architectural historian has termed Boyington "a prolific if undistinguished architect" best qualified to design railroad stations. Others have termed him an architect of great stature. Whatever his true talents, he was much in demand. After the 1871 fire, he spent decades building new edifices to replace his damaged creations. One architectural history credited Boyington with eighteen significant buildings in Chicago from 1872 through 1893. But Boyington was not limiting himself to Chicago. Terrace Hill was evidence of that. So were the Register newspaper building on Fourth Street, the Arsenal building, and the Des Moines Second Ward Schoolhouse, a three-story structure on Tenth Street between Mulberry and Cherry streets. It was built in the late 1860s at a cost of $80,000. Boyington was also the architect for the Central Presbyterian Church in Des Moines, begun in 1866. Allen, it so happened, was chairman of the church's building committee. Elsewhere in Iowa, Boyington designed the Council Bluffs mansion of Gen. Grenville Dodge, the railroad magnate who was a political ally of Allen's. The Dodge house is today a historic site open for public tours. Boyington drew the plans for churches in Iowa locales other than Des Moines, as well as in Indiana, Michigan, Ohio, Pennsylvania, and Wisconsin. He also designed secular buildings in such cities as Denver, Milwaukee, and Montreal. As the years passed, Allen retained Boyington to do other work—it is likely that the two men were in touch with one another even after Allen's financial demise and his move to California. There is evidence that the two men had more than an employer-employee relationship, that they became friends.

As Boyington's work at the Terrace Hill site progressed during 1867, the proposed mansion was understandably a topic of conversation. The April 28, 1867, *Daily State Register* said "the residence will be built and his grounds fitted up immediately." The architect had plans to make the residence and grounds "equal to anything west of New York," it was reported. The newspaper had no hesitation in letting local pride show: "When all the work is completed, Des Moines can invite the residents of her older sisters to come and see a specimen of what nature and skill and wealth can accomplish."

Just two weeks later, on May 12, 1867, the *Daily State*

Register again reported on the construction. After a look at Boyington's designs, the editor heightened his praise (and perhaps his hyperbole): "We find ourselves in attempting to describe this building under the necessity of changing the title from a villa to that of a stately mansion, as no less title would convey an adequate impression of it." The article provided what might have been the earliest public version of how the house itself would look: "The style of architecture is modern, or Americanized Italian, with a Mansard roof, giving the varied outline a most pleasing and picturesque appearance. . . . The approach through the meandering carriage drive will expose the stately, imposing tower on the north front, as well as the prominent turret on the east front, together with the numerous octagonal and circular projections, and the bracketed balconies and canopies on the various positions must impress the mind with the magnitude of the building."

The article also provided a glimpse of many interior features. From the main entrance, the visitor would enter a "richly furnished vestibule" and from there walk into the main hall. After that, there was magnificence at every turn, according to the article. On one side of the hall was a "drawing room of large dimensions," connected with the hall by large folding doors. The drawing room led into the library, a room which was becoming de rigeur in Victorian mansions of wealthy families at about that time. Nicolas Bentley, a commentator on the Victorian period, has said a library seemed essential to the master of such a household, "whether he was intellectually inclined or not." Bentley compared having a library then with the status inherent in having a swimming pool today.

After the newspaper article noted the library, it took the reader to the grand stairway, "located in a hall ten feet wide." There was also a more private side entrance to the east, uniting with the main hall. The library could be entered from this side hall; directly opposite were the family sitting room and the billiards room. Billiards was just becoming popular in the 1860s, so a billiards room was uncommon when Terrace Hill was constructed. At the east end of the hall was the music room, which had large sliding doors leading into the drawing room and folding doors opening on the hall. The article praised the systematic arrangement of the mansion's interior, including a commodious dining room in the corner, fitted with a butler's pantry. From there, a servants' stairway would lead to the basement. A dumbwaiter reached from the basement to the attic. The plans showed the kitchen in the basement along with a laundry area, drying and airing rooms, storerooms, the heating plant, and a place for the servants to eat their meals.

Nothing would be spared on the upstairs chambers, either. They were described by the newspaper article as "large, and each supplied with a commodious dressing room and wardrobe, bathrooms, and all other modern conveniences, with a supply of hot and cold water throughout. The attic will also be finished into various apartments for the household convenience." Paint was to be avoided—hardwood was planned for throughout the mansion. Polished rosewood would be in evidence, too, in the first-floor doors. Other areas of the house would be in various woods, including oak, maple, and butternut. The exterior would be finished with brick and cut stone trimmings. The roof would be ornamental. Later newspaper articles described additional features, such as a suite of four mantels designed especially for the mansion by the Chicago firm of Sherman Cole and Co. Before the mantels were shipped to Des Moines, they were on display in Chicago, where the *Chicago Republican* described them as "exquisite." The article noted that "connoisseurs and practical mechanics who have seen them unite in according them the praise of being superb in workmanship, as well as models in beauty of design." The mantels were in bold relief, with the one for the drawing room "of pure snowy statuary marble, in the medallion style." That one mantel cost $1,000, not including statues of Prayer and Water Nymph that would sit on top of it. The mantel for the parlor was "of dainty and chaste design." The dining room and library mantels were of Spanish marble, relieved with black marble ornaments. The parlor, dining room, and library mantels were estimated to cost $500 apiece.

The "elegant stair work" for Terrace Hill was done by Foster Brothers, a Des Moines manufacturer with a factory on Mulberry Street. The steam heating apparatus was assembled by Northwestern Manufacturing Co. of Chicago. At times attention was focused more on the workers than on their handiwork. For example, on November 15, 1867, the *Daily State Register* reported that painter A. B. Bender had fallen fifty feet to the ground while working on the Terrace Hill tower. It was feared that he was injured seriously, but six days later he was back on his feet.

The mansion itself was not the only building going up on the vast grounds. The first structure to be completed, according to Allen's recollections in 1876, was the gardener's house. It was ready for occupancy in the spring of 1868. Allen said it had cost $1,600. It was the only building for which he kept a separate account. Allen was unable to say precisely what Terrace Hill cost, because he had lumped expenses such as materials for the barn and greenhouse in with the mansion. Construction of all the buildings was proceeding well in 1868 under the supervision of George Whitaker. He had been a contractor in Des Moines since 1857, and had worked with Allen and Boyington on other projects. While the work proceeded, Allen was broadening his commercial activities. Railroading especially received his attention. On October 31, 1867, Allen was appointed by a judge as receiver in a legal struggle. The parties were the giant Chicago, Rock Island and Pacific Railroad on one side, the tiny Mississippi and Missouri on the other. The M&M, begun in 1853, had never reached Iowa's western border, despite its optimistic name. It had barely got west of Iowa City when in 1866 the Rock Island took over the financially ailing line for $5.5 million. The M&M was planning to distribute those proceeds to its stockholders, without paying its creditors. The creditors were unhappy with that arrangement and filed a lawsuit. Allen's job was to manage the assets carefully until the legal tangle could be resolved. The assets turned over to him consisted of 541 bonds of $1,000 each, plus about $100,000 in cash. What Allen did with those assets will be detailed later in this book; suffice it to say here that he did not conserve the fund. He was never punished for his mismanagement, but in the end he paid dearly, because the squandered assets were to play a major role in Allen's demise.

The trust fund was not the only tie between Allen and the powerful Rock Island line. He was buying land along existing and probable routes from Davenport to Council Bluffs, then selling the parcels at a profit. Allen had excellent opportunities to gain inside information because he was a stockholder and corporate director of the Rock Island. The importance of lines such as the Rock Island to the economy of the nation and of Iowa can hardly be overestimated. Although Allen and others had begun pushing for railroads throughout Iowa as early as 1849, by the mid-1860s many cities, including Des Moines, still lacked direct service. Without it, producers and consumers were "hopelessly separated," as the *Davenport Gazette* put it in early 1866: "The great need of central and western Iowa today is railroads. For want of these, thousands of Iowa farmers find their stores of golden grain practically valueless, and all the rich fruits of their smiling harvests turned to ashes. To induce, stimulate, and aid the building of railroads, our interior counties have for months past been kept in a fever of railroad excitement. Meetings have been held, conventions called, subscriptions pleaded for, surveys undertaken, and companies organized, and all for one great object—to build railroads where now the sole routes of intercommunications are the wagon track and open prairie."

While Allen benefitted by being an insider in this railroad boom, he continued to embark on non-railroading enterprises. One was to have a heavy bearing on Terrace Hill, although neither Allen nor anyone else could have guessed it at the start. The enterprise was the Equitable Life Insurance Co. of Iowa. Allen was a key figure in its formation during 1867, although Frederick Marion Hubbell was the guiding force. Allen and Hubbell had known each other for at least six years prior to the founding of the insurance company, and they might have know one another as early as 1855. After the formation of Equitable Life Insurance, their paths crossed often, sometimes daily, for seventeen years. It was at that juncture that Hubbell became the master of Terrace Hill, the mansion which Allen had so proudly built. The way that Equitable Life fit in was that by 1884, thanks in large part to the success of the insurance company, Hubbell had amassed enough wealth to make owning Terrace Hill feasible.

Chapter Three

Young Hubbell

When Frederick Hubbell arrived in Fort Des Moines from Connecticut in 1855, he was sixteen. He was ten years younger than B.F. Allen, who was already well-established in Fort Des Moines as a landbuyer and banker. It did not take Hubbell long to catch up with Allen, however. And as it turned out, Hubbell had more staying power at the top. Although Hubbell, like Allen, had setbacks in his business career and personal life, his story, unlike Allen's, was one of nearly unbroken success. Despite their different fates, something ties the two men inextricably together. That something is Terrace Hill.

When Hubbell got off the stagecoach in Fort Des Moines on May 7, 1855, he did not intend to stay long. He had come with his father Francis because his father wanted to speculate in land, and Iowa seemed like a good spot from everything that was said back East. There was no indication that Frederick would settle in Iowa—his goal was to attend the U.S. Military Academy at West Point. Hubbell already had completed what today would be termed a high school education, making him a well-educated youth for that time and place.

Francis B. Hubbell, a stonemason and farmer by trade, did not waste time upon arriving in Fort Des Moines. He traveled outside of the settlement to look for land that the federal government was selling for $1.25 an acre. Frederick stayed in town and found a job at the U.S. Land Office. Doing the hiring was Phineas M. Casady, a lawyer and early settler at Fort Des Moines who was receiver of public monies in the land office. Settlers claiming land had to pay in gold. Casady was responsible for getting the funds to the federal subtreasury office in Saint Louis. Sometimes he carried the funds himself, taking a stagecoach to Keokuk, Iowa, and then a steamboat down the Mississippi River.

Casady was not certain why he hired Hubbell, a mere boy, and small in stature (about five feet, two inches) at that. As recreated by historian George Sexton Pease, Casady thought upon hearing Hubbell's request for a job: ''I told him I couldn't use a green boy, but he said he'd learn. I asked him what he thought he could do, and he said he could show me better than tell me. I asked how much he wanted, and he said that was up to me. So I asked about his schooling, and found out he had studied Latin and knew algebra and geometry. Those seemed to be pretty high qualifications for an office boy, so I told him to come to work in the morning.'' Hubbell's wages were $8.33 a month plus board. Some historians have looked at that and concluded Hubbell was a poverty-stricken youth. Such an image made for a good Horatio Alger twist when Hubbell ended up to be a multimillionnaire. But the image of Hubbell as poverty-stricken does not fit the facts. His father had enough money to travel to Iowa, buy land, and travel back to Connecticut. Furthermore, after 1855, Francis Burritt Hubbell made numerous trips to Iowa. He was a stonemason so talented that his skills were in demand not only in the East but also in the Midwest and West.

Francis Burritt Hubbell.

Frederick did not become rich working in the land office, but he learned a lesson there that was one of the most important of his career: Land was money. Land speculation held a fascination for Hubbell, just as it did for B.F. Allen. In the long run, however, Hubbell's conservatism and shrewd business sense led him to a permanent position at the top, whereas Allen's capricious, gambling nature plummeted him to bankruptcy. The land office in 1855 was doing a booming business. Shortly after starting, Hubbell took in $15,000 in one day. An early recorder was his father, who bought 1,600 acres in Dallas County, then quickly sold the land at a 40 percent profit. Soon Francis was on his way back to Connecticut to his wife Augusta Church Hubbell. Frederick, though, decided to stay in Iowa. Within a year, he followed the frontier west from Fort Des Moines to Sioux City. The land office in Fort Des Moines was about to close, and Casady suggested that his clerk follow opportunity to where the land was not so settled. Hubbell listened. He spent most of the next five years helping organize northwest Iowa, building the beginnings of his own fortune along the way.

Much is known of Hubbell's years in what had been an uncharted region from the detailed diaries he kept. The diaries were begun on Hubbell's journey from Connecticut to Iowa. There were occasional gaps in the entries, including one break after Hubbell's departure from Fort Des Moines for Sioux City on March 4, 1856. The break continued after his arrival in Sioux City nine days later. (Today the trip takes fewer than four hours by interstate highway.) When the diary entries resumed on April 21, Hubbell noted that he had recorded 640 acres of land. He was just seventeen years old. The youth induced his father to return to Iowa to help with the land-buying, because a person under twenty-one years of age could not legally claim land. Francis Hubbell arrived in Sioux City on July 6, 1856. "Father and I went over to the claim and slept there, as it was necessary for us to live on the land," Hubbell's diary said. "Mosquitoes are very thick. Could not sleep any. Had a rain in the night. Got wet."

Hubbell did not hold onto all the land he recorded in Sioux City, knowing that there was quick money to be made. For example, on October 22, 1856, he bought a town lot for an unrecorded price, then sold it the same day for $400. While engaged in landbuying Hubbell realized, in the pragmatic American tradition, that knowing law would be useful. He threw himself into the study of the subject, and by April 1858 Hubbell was admitted to the practice of law in Iowa. He was nineteen. The *Sioux City Eagle* commented, "Mr. Hubbell is a young man of good abilities and possesses those qualities which will insure success."

Entrepreneur that he was, Hubbell opened a business in 1857 as a general land agent. The October 10, 1857, *Sioux City Eagle* carried an advertisement under Hubbell's name that read: "Land located for settlers or distant dealers at lowest rates. Land and town lots bought and sold on commission.

Land warrants bought and sold. Land warrants and money loaned at western rates of interest." Even before becoming an agent, Hubbell had amassed at least a modest fortune, especially for somebody so young. By year-end 1856 his diary recorded ownership of 13½ town lots valued at $240 each, plus 40 acres of rural land valued at $20 an acre. It did not come without some anguish, however. The diary reported: "I have labored during the past year exceeding hard and it has been a species of labor that is wearisome in the extreme—that of living in a new country, undergoing hardships and disadvantages of the same, constantly harassed with this one absorbing thought that if one should be sick or other calamity befall him that he has no resources of his own, nor true and tried friends on whom he can rely for assistance in time of need."

The next year, 1857, brought companionship in the person of Mary Wilkins, Sioux City's first schoolteacher, a twenty-year-old from Keosauqua, Iowa. But that companionship eventually led to heartbreak for Hubbell. His diaries recorded the ups and downs of the romance. Probably the height of his optimism was in February 1858, when he wrote such phrases as "I am scarcely happy except when with her, which is pretty often lately. And I believe she enjoys my society as well as I do hers. . . .When I am of age I shall be ready to marry. The time will pass quickly and two years will try our loves. For my own part, I have no fears for the result." By April, though, Mary Wilkins was dating other men, and in August she was engaged to Charley Rustin, one of Hubbell's partners in land speculation. Hubbell made periodic trips back to Des Moines during his Sioux City years, before and after his romance with Mary Wilkins. Each time he wrestled with the question of remaining in Des Moines, where he wanted to practice law with Casady. Finally, in 1859, Hubbell departed Sioux City for good. But he did not go back to Des Moines right away. He traveled north into the uncharted land of Sioux County, Iowa. The activities of Hubbell there were not recorded in detail, because his annual diaries stopped at the end of 1858, or else were misplaced. It was not until twenty-two years later that any known diaries resumed.

Hubbell was one of the early Caucasian settlers in Sioux County. In February 1860 the first election was held there. Four votes were cast, one of them being Hubbell's, and he became clerk of the district court. It was the only time he was to hold an elected public office. As a county official, Hubbell worked hard to make the area habitable. After eighteen months there, however, he had had enough. By mid-1861 he was back in Des Moines, working as a law clerk in the office of Casady and Jefferson S. Polk. The return of Hubbell was the start of a seventy-year reign as one of the city's most influential citizens. Within a few decades, he was certainly the city's wealthiest person, and probably the wealthiest in Iowa. By then he was living in Iowa's premier residence—Terrace Hill. But long before that, in 1862, Hubbell had arrived in his own estimation. That was because he had saved $1,200 to buy a partnership in the Casady and Polk law firm. He also did some courting. His affections were aimed first at Caroline Florence Cooper, a beauty who was a daughter of Des Moines pioneer Isaac Cooper and a grand-niece of author James Fenimore Cooper. The young lawyer Hubbell proposed marriage to Florence, but was rejected. Simpson Smith, who knew Hubbell in F.M.'s later years, related that Florence believed her suitor "would never amount to much." She married instead a Mr. Ginn, who Smith said, never did amount to much. Hubbell was undaunted. In 1863, he proposed marriage to Florence's sister Frances, with whom he had been friends for years. Her name appeared in his diary while he was in northwest Iowa. Frances did not reject Hubbell. The *Daily State Register* on March 21, 1863, carried this notice of the wedding: "Married, on the nineteenth at the residence of the bride's father, by Rev. Thompson Bird, F.M. Hubbell, Esq., and Miss Frances E. Cooper, all of this city. Our best wishes go with the happy pair. The nineteenth day of March, although stormy and dark and dismal to most folks, brought sunshine and happiness to our young friends. May that sunshine and that happiness remain with them forever!" The marriage was to continue—

Isaac Cooper. (Courtesy Iowa State Historical Department.)

happily, it appears—for sixty-one years until Mrs. Hubbell's death. Frederick and Frances lived with her parents at first, in the Cooper home at Fifth and Sycamore streets. In 1865, the Hubbell family—which by then included a son, Frederick Cooper Hubbell—moved into a newly built home not far from the in-laws. Family life was not interrupted by the Civil War, because Hubbell, like Allen, did not serve in the military. Instead, he stayed in Des Moines and began building a financial empire based on real estate, railroads, and insurance.

The real estate habit, of course, had been established early, from the time Hubbell arrived in Iowa. One historian wrote later of Hubbell in the mid-1860s: "F.M. believed the way to get rich was to acquire property and let the growth of the community increase its value, and his judgment told him that Des Moines was destined to grow." Hubbell had the foresight to know in which direction Des Moines would grow, too. He bought land where his instincts told him to buy, and he was proven correct. At the time, the main business district consisted of five blocks along Court Avenue. But Hubbell bought lots on Locust Avenue and on High, Walnut, and Sycamore streets, believing that Court Avenue would run out of choice locations. Hubbell acquired lots outside the business district as well. By the time a railroad reached Des Moines in 1866, Hubbell owned much of the land where the rails were laid. The following year, when the giant Rock Island line reached Des Moines, Hubbell controlled parcels that railroad wanted. His first personal fling with railroading was on a small scale. With his partner Polk and two other men, Hubbell obtained the street railway charter in Des Moines. The line started at the Polk County courthouse and extended to the foot of the Capitol. The passenger cars were drawn by horses. That was the same year, 1866, in which Hubbell decided to form a life insurance company, an entity that was to have a major effect on Hubbell and on Terrace Hill.

Here was how the thought came to Hubbell, as recounted by Phineas Casady in George Sexton Pease's company-sponsored history of Equitable Life: "Mat Dickinson from Keokuk, I think it was, got Fred interested in life insurance when he tried to sell him a policy in New York's Mutual Life. Fred had never heard of legal reserve life insurance, but something Mat said aroused that big bump of curiosity of his. After spending an afternoon of explanation, Mat remembered a book containing all sorts of tables written by some mathematician back East. So he sent for the book, and told Fred to read it." Hubbell devoured the book. Life insurance seemed an almost fail-safe way to make money. A company had to earn 4 percent on its funds. Iowans, short of capital for developing the state, were willing to pay 10 percent. The 6 percent differential looked good to Hubbell.

There were already property insurance companies in Des Moines—the Hawkeye, organized in March 1865 by Allen and others, and the State, organized later that year. But there were no life insurance companies. On January 21, 1867,

Horse-drawn streetcar, which traveled from the Courthouse to the Capitol. (Courtesy Paul K. Ashby.)

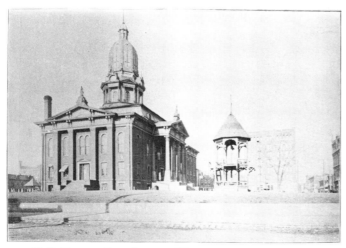

Polk County Courthouse. (Courtesy Paul K. Ashby.)

Hubbell convened a meeting to fill the void. It was held in the Sherman business block, at the office used by Casady and his associate James Tuttle for their Iowa Land Co. Hubbell had called together the business elite of the community. He himself was the youngest, having just turned twenty-eight. Prominent among the men was Allen, already the state's leading banker at age thirty-seven. Others at the meeting included many who would play roles in the lives of Allen and Hubbell: Hoyt Sherman, pioneer lawyer, banker, and member of an esteemed family that included a U.S. senator, a Civil War general, and a federal judge; Hoyt's brother Lampson, who edited one of the earliest Des Moines newspapers and served as mayor; Jefferson Polk, Hubbell's law and business partner; Isaac Cooper, a building contractor and Hubbell's father-in-law; Francis West, a banker and Allen's father-in-law; Henry L. Whitman, M.D.; James B. Stewart, banker and real estate broker; James C. Jordan, cattlebreeder and fervent abolitionist; Peter Myers, publisher, real estate broker, and auctioneer; William W. Williamson, judge, editor, and politician; Robert L. Tidrick, a lawyer who had served as the town's first schoolmaster; Wesley Redhead, developer of coal mines; Casady and Tuttle.

The men accepted the idea of a life insurance company after an explanation from Hoyt Sherman; Hubbell was not one for doing much talking. When the election of officers took place, Hubbell was not nominated. But that was by his own design. He feared his youthfulness would hurt the acceptance of the company. As a result, he had prevailed upon the venerable Casady to be the first Equitable Life Insurance Co. of Iowa president. Allen was elected treasurer. Hubbell took the title of secretary, and Hoyt Sherman became actuary-manager. Hubbell and Sherman would run the company from day to day.

Four days after the meeting, the group reassembled to sign the articles of incorporation. The founders then applied for insurance coverage for themselves, to put customers on the books. Hubbell was first, buying a $2,000 policy payable to his wife Frances. The articles of incorporation were filed February 6, 1867, and the next day an advertisement appeared in the newspapers. The main office was listed at No. 4, Sherman Block. A portion of the advertisement read "Policies issued on as favorable terms as any other solvent and reliable company. Money to loan on real estate primarily. Apply to F.M. Hubbell, secretary." The list of the company's founders was impressive enough—as Hubbell had hoped it would be—that one newspaper commented, "A glance at the names affixed to the advertisement is all that is necessary to show the stability of the company." By the end of 1867 the company had $210,700 of life insurance in force, and had collected premiums of $17,459. It did not seem like an auspicious beginning, perhaps, for what was to become the keystone of Hubbell's fortune, the same fortune that was used to buy, improve, and maintain Terrace Hill. But the growth of Equitable Life would come in time.

Equitable Life could have played a major role in Allen's

fortune, too. In 1872 he became the second president, succeeding Casady. Life insurance had never been Casady's main interest—in fact, when he resigned he got out altogether by selling his stock to Hubbell. Great things were expected of Allen. Pease's company history said: "Allen had never known the taste of defeat. His had been a scintillating saga of success when he was elected president of Equitable of Iowa on May 24, 1872. Had he been content to remain master of Terrace Hill, had he elected to make his office the platform from which to rule his domain, the history of the company might have followed a wholly different course. It was not to be." By January 1874 Allen had stepped down as Equitable Life's president. He was nearly bankrupt, although not many people suspected that. Within a year, the world would know. Until 1874, however, Allen put on the face of a successful millionaire, as he basked in the glory of the monument he had built—Terrace Hill.

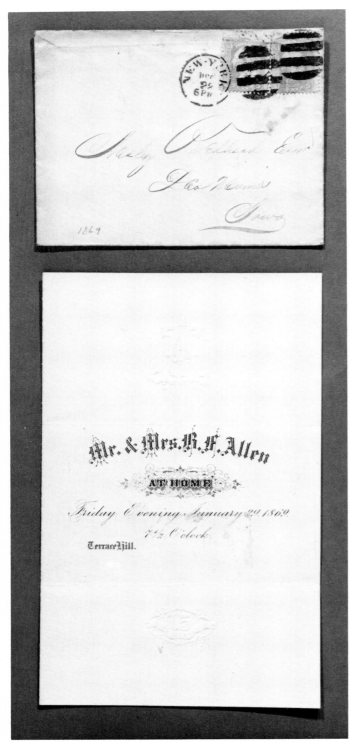

Open house invitation sent by B. F. and Arathusa Allen in 1869. (From the Wesley Redhead Collection owned by Herbert K. Redhead, Bentonsport, Iowa.)

Chapter Four

The Dream
and the Debacle

Benjamin and Arathusa Allen opened Terrace Hill to their friends on January 29, 1869, their fifteenth wedding anniversary. Their former home at Fourth and Court had been sold for $28,000, and was to become the site of the Aborn House, a well-known hotel. The Allens had moved into Terrace Hill during the summer of 1868. The mansion was more glamorous (or ostentatious, depending on the point of view) than any other residence in Iowa. The party was in keeping with the mansion's character. More than 1,000 invitations were mailed, some to New York City. Chicago was represented by at least a dozen guests, including Boyington, the mansion's architect. Three Chicago newspapers sent reporters to cover the event, as did one in Indianapolis. Among the Iowa dignitaries attending were Gov. Samuel Merrill, Congressman-elect Frank Palmer, and judges from the state Supreme Court.

The food was served at 10 P.M. in the dining hall. It had been prepared by John Wright, who was brought in from the Opera House Restaurant in Chicago. The meal reportedly cost the Allens $6,000, which would probably be over $40,000 in today's currency. A sampling of the menu suggested why. There were two fruitcakes weighing twenty-five pounds each, ice cream molded in the figure of George Washington, a twenty-five pound lady cake, oysters, boned turkeys in colored jellies, and a variety of meats. Flowers were everywhere. They had cost about $2,000, with the bouquet at the center of the long dinner table accounting for $700. That would be the equivalent of paying $4,000 or more for a floral centerpiece today. Entertainment was provided by two players alternating at the Allens' grand piano, accompanied by singers. There was also a vocal performance by Kitty, the Allens' eldest daughter.

The praise for the gala event was generous, and not just from local residents. The *Chicago Republican,* for example, published an article on the party at the "costly suburban palace" which said that the distinguished assemblage of guests did not overshadow the house itself. Terrace Hill was termed "one of the finest, most costly, and tastefully completed private residences in the country." The bulk of the *Republican's* compliments, though, were reserved for Allen himself: "The worthy host is one of the selfmade men, who, in this free land, by virtue of untiring energy, far-seeing sagacity, and unquestioned integrity has in comparatively few years risen from moderate circumstances to a position of wealth and independence, exercising controlling influence in behalf of his chosen city and state." Allen's wealth was estimated at between $3 million and $4 million, but it had not gone to his head, according to the *Republican* article. Rather, Allen was described as "unostentatious, courteous, and affable."

The *Daily State Register* also had nothing but compliments for Allen. The *Register* termed him "as public-spirited as he is energetic. His whole course upward has been marked with countless evidence that his ambition has been as great to build up Des Moines as it was to raise himself. The good he has worked for the city is beyond estimation." The cost of the mansion and the furnishings was generally estimated at $250,000, although some estimates were as high as $400,000. Whatever, the cost, the money had built a house holding hundreds of guests comfortably. The *Register* noted: "The large company, which in the largest of residences would have been packed and crowded beyond comfort's point, in the large and roomy apartments of this palace found no discomfort. There was room in abundance, and the ladies could promenade free from fear of the blundering footfalls of awkward men disturbing their sweeping trains." But beyond the idolatry of wealth, the newspaper accounts provided the most detailed description available of the mansion. The furniture was designed expressly for Terrace Hill by J. Ziegler and Co. of New York City. Advertisements for that firm said that all of its furniture was made by craftsmen who specialized in the "latest and most fashionable patterns." The member of the Ziegler company coming to Des Moines to oversee placement of the furniture was H.C. Glinsmann, known not only as a decorator but also as an inventor of a table with a number of special functions.

The carpets and the curtains were manufactured in New York City also, by A.T. Stewarts. Details gleaned from newspaper accounts showed why the house attracted attention: The front door, 12½ feet high, led through a vestibule to the main hall, fifteen feet wide and nearly fifteen feet high. The south half of the main hall broadened to accommodate the grand staircase. An auxiliary hall led from the music room to the east porch, bisecting the main hall. The main hall floor was made of walnut and oak, over which was spread a Wilton carpet. On the right side of the east hall was a walnut apparel stand with brass hat hooks, topped with Lisbon marble, over which was a six-foot by nine-foot mirror. At the intersection of the two halls were five-foot-high carved alabaster vases. The drawing room, off the hall, contained furniture "in the ancient Grecian style," consisting of two sofas, two armchairs, four sitting chairs, two reception chairs, two crinoline chairs, two French bebe chairs, two bronze statues on pedestals, two flower stands, a cabinet inlaid with various kinds of wood in mosaic, a mantel mirror finished in rosewood, and a center table elaborately ornamented on the top and sides. The table had cost about $1,000 and was termed "the richest piece of work of its kind in this country." The drawing room had curtains of heavy crimson satin. Car-

Walnut hall tree and umbrella stand; probably the only original Allen piece of furniture remaining in Terrace Hill today.

Detail of hall tree brass hat hooks in the shape of the phoenix—emblem of immortality.

pets of the Axminster variety had been made especially for the room.

Adjoining the drawing room to the south was the music room, which contained a Chickering Louis XIV grand piano. The library room, also opening off the hall, contained cases of French walnut with plate glass doors topped by bronze statues. (The library in 1869 was not located where the library of Terrace Hill is today, if newspaper accounts are trustworthy. Today's library occupies the area where the billiards room used to be, next to the sitting room to the southeast of the grand stair. The reception room today is located where the original library was.) The furniture included six armchairs, a black and green tapestry, and a table. A large mirror was on the east side, corresponding with a mirror on the west side of the drawing room. The two mirrors created an effect of "magnificent distance" when somebody stood between them. The carpet was a Wilton, in one piece. South of the library was the sitting room, which contained yet another large mirror. Opposite the sitting room was the dining room. The French walnut sideboard in it was ornamented with carved seahorses, Grecian heads, and topped by Lisbon marble, according to a newspaper account. The sideboard as viewed in Terrace Hill today has no Grecian heads or seahorses carved on it, raising questions about the accuracy of the description. The stairway at the south end of the hall led to the northeast bedroom on the second floor. There was a bedstead, bureau, mirror, statuary marble mantel, commode, a table inlaid with various woods, a lounge, four chairs, a rocker, and a French secretary. Other bedrooms were furnished in equally lavish style. The southeast room was the upstairs family room. Attached to it was a nursery and a bathroom. A system of call bells interconnected all parts of the mansion.

Terrace Hill, depending on one's viewpoint, was either a home of elegant good taste or a symbol of America's nouveau riche class that garishly displayed the wealth made possible by a young industrial democracy. Whatever one's viewpoint, the romantic legend of Terrace Hill was launched. Benjamin Allen was not quite forty years old, and in good health. Arathusa was even younger. There was every reason to think they would reign over Terrace Hill for decades. Who would have guessed that in six years Allen's angry creditors would be fighting over the mansion, that in eight years Arathusa would be dead, that in fifteen years F.M. Hubbell—one of the less notable guests at the party—would be the owner of Terrace Hill? In 1869, though, all seemed well. The next year's U.S. Census showed the Allens with four children, eight servants living in the mansion, and multimillionaire status. The family was a close-knit one. In the autumn of 1869 they made a trip to New York to drop off Kitty at Vassar College. The pet dog went, too, but died on the return to Des Moines, upsetting Arathusa. As Allen recalled, "It laid so still in the basket, and when we took it out to eat it would not. My wife did all she could for it, and almost cried when it died."

But even momentary sadness was rare in those years. Allen's vast business interests appeared healthy. The *Des Moines City Directory and Business Guide* for 1869 showed Allen as president of three banks; later that year, he became president of the newly formed Capital City Bank. He was a director of two insurance companies and a narrow gauge railroad, and treasurer of the Des Moines Gas Co. The directory listings were not complete, either. Allen additionally was treasurer of the Hawkeye Insurance Co. and the Des Moines Petroleum and Mining Co. He was a director of the Rock Island Railroad and a key figure in a Rock Island-related land company. Allen soon became president of the newly organized Des Moines and Minnesota Railroad Co., an organizer of the Des Moines Water Co., president of the Des Moines division of

the Chicago-based Republic Life Insurance Co., the primary creditor of the *Daily State Register* (because of a $25,000 loan to the Clarkson family, which used the money to purchase the newspaper), a major stockholder in Equitable Life (by obtaining shares from other founders who were unable to keep up with their assessments), and the holder of at least $75,000 of Des Moines municipal bonds.

All the activity, however, was not as profitable as it appeared. As already noted, Allen was a plunger, and like plungers everywhere he was not always successful. An 1881 U.S. Supreme Court ruling involving Allen's bankruptcy cited his assets and liabilities in 1868, seven years before his bankruptcy and even before Terrace Hill was dedicated. The court said: "It is apparent that at the time mentioned he had little or no available capital of his own with which to carry on business. This state of affairs caused him to succumb to the temptation to use the (Mississippi and Missouri Railroad) trust assets in his possession as receiver. Towards the close of 1868 he had deposited a part of the Chicago, Rock Island and Pacific Railroad bonds which belonged to this trust fund with Gilman, Son and Co., bankers in the city of New York, and borrowed upon them, as collateral security, the sum of $55,000."

Allen's maneuverings to stay afloat were not known in 1869 when he ran for the Iowa Senate on the Republican ticket. Running for office was not Allen's own idea, but he was not hard to persuade. As Des Moines attorney C.C. Nourse recounted in a privately published autobiography, former Iowa Supreme Court Justice George Wright was running for the U.S. Senate in 1869 and wanted a friend from Polk County on whom he could depend in the Iowa Senate. Nourse suggested Allen's name to Wright, partly because of Allen's reputation as "the leading banker in western Iowa." There was another reason behind Nourse's thinking, too. Des Moines residents wanted money from the legislature for a new Capitol building, "and Mr. Allen by virtue of his influence through the western part of the state could probably do more than any other man to secure such an appropriation," Nourse wrote. On October 12, 1869, Allen was elected. Soon after that, he threw a party at Terrace Hill to electioneer for the new Capitol. John Kasson, a state legislator who had been and would again be a U.S. congressman, was for the new Capitol himself, and was pleased to have Allen among the supporters. Writing in 1900, Kasson reflected: "Allen was then a prosperous and influential banker widely known in the state, and an old settler. He was no speaker, but perhaps on that account better adapted to conciliate the Senate by his pleasant manners and practical good sense."

Allen became deeply involved in politics. In the 1871 race for governor of Iowa, Allen was mentioned as a candidate. He declined. But Allen did work for the election of C.C. Carpenter as governor and for the candidacy of William B. Allison as U.S. senator. The Republicans were worried that Allison would lose, especially if the *Daily State Register* supported Allison's

Sen. B. F. Allen, elected in 1869. (Courtesy Iowa State Historical Department.)

foe. In 1870, the Clarkson family—father Coker, son James (Ret), and son Richard—had purchased the *Register* for $30,000, of which $25,000 was lent by Allen. Ret and Richard leaned towards Allison, but not Coker. Something had to be done. It was. According to historian Stanley P. Hirshson, ''to make sure the *Register* did not cause trouble at a vital moment, B.F. Allen and (Gen. Grenville) Dodge bought Coker Clarkson's interest in the paper for $19,000.'' After Allison's victory, his defeated opponent James Harlan complained about Allen's influence. In a letter to a supporter, Harlan said, ''The *Register* was indebted to B.F. Allen for $25,000 on the purchase price of that establishment. It was understood at Des Moines that Mr. Allison advanced $5,000 which had matured on the debt, at about the date of its first onslaught on me. . . . The *(Register's)* management of the campaign . . . was, as I think, most disreputable.'' Allen served in the Iowa Senate into 1873. His activities were controversial. In February 1873 the *Des Moines Republican*, a rival to the pro-Allen *Register*, published an anonymous letter charging Allen with disbursing $68,000 in 1872 to legislators to defeat proposals disliked by the railroads. Allen denied the accusations, so the Senate appointed an investigating committee. Testimony was taken from numerous witnesses, including former Gov. Samuel Merrill, at that time a banking rival of Allen. Witnesses told damning stories about Allen, then later recanted. Merrill eventually admitted that the anonymous letter was filled with false charges. Allen, who may indeed have had something to hide, quickly suggested that the inquiry be dropped. The Senate obliged. The affair was ended, having raised more questions than it answered.

If Allen did pay money to legislators on behalf of railroad interests, it would not have been the only time. In 1868, a year before Allen was elected to the Senate, he paid at least $500 to John Kasson as a conduit for the Rock Island Railroad. That payment was revealed during the trial of an 1875 libel lawsuit filed by Kasson against *Register* publisher Ret Clarkson and others.

Allen's involvement in politics did not mean the neglect of Terrace Hill. He was as proud of it as could be. It was in the news regularly. Sometimes the house was the site of weddings involving people married there simply so they could say they had been married there. For example, on May 2, 1871, Paul F. Shorer and Mary A. Cooney were wed at Terrace Hill. On August 7, 1869, the house was opened for a different purpose —to give astronomers a vantage point from which to view a total eclipse of the sun. Outsiders also came to Terrace Hill to buy flowers. The keeper of the Allens' hothouse just south of the mansion advertised when he had flowers for sale. The mansion was expensive to maintain in those early years, just as it would be later. One journalist reported that it cost $27,000 in upkeep in 1870. But it seemed as if there were no end to Allen's wealth, so the expense did not raise many eyebrows.

Despite seeming affluence, however, Allen was not a carefree man. He was borrowing money from the railroad bond fund in his trust, and he worried about how he would pay it back when the court asked for an accounting. Instead of facing the problem, Allen continued to speculate, working to postpone the day of reckoning before the judge. The *Chicago Tribune* years later published quotations from an alleged diary kept by Allen. Many of the entries were about the bond fund. Allen denied any diaries existed. But he did not deny the quotations themselves, which were in fact taken from ''confidential'' letters written to his New York City banking cohorts Herman Blennerhassett and W.A. Stephens. Allen knew that some of his correspondence was damning: In 1874, before the *Tribune* article appeared, he asked a New York City stockbroker to destroy letters that had passed between the two men. The *Tribune* noted that ''A banker even of the most desperate class is apt to regard a trust fund as a sacred charge, a something upon which not the direst personal necessity can sanction or extenuate approach. . . . Your reputable and discreet banker always puts his trust money in an easily convertible shape. The securities in which he invests it are those which can be transmuted into cash at the shortest notice.'' But, the *Tribune* said, Allen ''certainly did not regard the half million dollars of Mississippi and Missouri Railroad money in any such delicate fashion. He put the deposit where he thought it would do the most good to himself personally, and when the day of settlement came, that mortal inability to redeem his faith struck him all at once.''

The *Tribune* published one passage allegedly written by Allen on September 29, 1871. It read in part: ''My means are so scattered and collections so slow that it will take some time for me to get my means in proper shape. I am getting ready to settle with the parties interested in the railroad fund which I have been holding as receiver for some time. As the fund is quite large it will take all my available funds, coming as it will in my busiest season. . . .When I have this receiver fund settled up, I shall have nothing to trouble me.'' Allen felt alternately optimistic and pessimistic about having to repay the court soon. For example, on April 29, 1872, he congratulated himself about the judge not having ordered a settlement of the fund. But on May 8, Allen wrote, ''I had begun to feel pretty sanguine it would go over another term, but it could not be delayed any longer. My attorney has several schemes for delay, but it is not safe to depend on and the only prudent course is to get ready to settle.'' Whether the Allen quotations were completely accurate was academic, because the 1881 U.S. Supreme Court decision left no doubt that Allen was wheeling and dealing with trust fund money. The court said that more than once, Allen pledged all the bonds to secure loans for himself, generally from brokers in New York City. Before he was able to obtain those loans, Allen often had to agree to pay interest at an extra-high rate; the brokers knew that they had him over a barrel. As the Supreme Court phrased it, by mid-1873 ''Allen was in a desperate strait and resorted to desperate means to save himself.'' Those means will be recounted later in this narrative. They were to have a profound effect on Allen and his creditors. They were also to have a profound effect on the future of Terrace Hill.

Meanwhile, Allen continued his businesses in Des Moines and elsewhere. His clients, bank depositors, friends, and possibly even his family remained blissfully unaware of the coming collapse. Allen had expanded his already broad base by opening a bank in 1872 in New York City. His partners were Stephens and Blennerhassett, both of whom had worked for a New York bond house that handled some of the receiver's fund Rock Island securities. The bank flourished from the start, although trouble was almost certain to overtake it because of the manner of its establishment. As an 1878 court ruling put it, the three partners ''commenced business without a dollar of actual capital, and in fact paid for the fixtures and furniture of the house out of their depositors' money. Allen was the only person of reputed respectability in the firm, and he was then without a doubt in a state of commercial insolvency. The other members of the firm, Stephens and Blennerhassett, were without means of capital.'' The New York bank advertised in Iowa, taking advantage of the trust in Allen's name. One advertisement in a Des Moines newspaper said, ''Have organized a domestic banking business in New York City, with a department especially devoted to the care of out-of-town accounts, and can attend to them better than the incorporated banks of the city, which are organized more for city business. Four percent allowed on daily balances. Accounts rendered and credited monthly. All orders to buy or sell stocks on speculation positively declined. Can sell good bonds of cities, counties, states, etc., but they must be first-class. Every kind of legitimate banking business done.''

Immediately below that advertisement was one for the National State Bank in Des Moines, B.F. Allen president. The text referred to the National State Bank's correspondent arrangement with Allen, Stephens and Co., and a correspondent arrangement with Cook County National Bank, which Allen also owned by then. The Des Moines-Chicago-New York City ties were looked upon favorably in Iowa—at least until Allen's downfall—rather than considered to be a conflict of interests. In January 1874 a Des Moines newspaper lauded the growth of local banking, noting that in December 1873 alone the National State Bank and B.F. Allen's private bank did more than $1 million of business with Allen's Chicago and New York institutions.

Besides expanding his banking business outside Iowa, Allen was forever becoming involved in other new ventures. Often he was accompanied by the cream of the Des Moines business community, including F.M. Hubbell. In 1872, Allen was an incorporator of the Des Moines and Northwestern Railroad Co. By that time, he also owned the property of the Des Moines Gas Co. and 100 percent of its stock. He invested $190,000 in the New York State Loan and Trust Co. in an unsuccessful attempt to gain control. He was a force in the Chicago and Pacific Railroad being constructed from Chicago through its suburbs. Still other ventures included a $35,000 investment in Wesley Redhead's Black Diamond Coal Mine on Des Moines' south side, an interest in a firm publishing state atlases, and a role in the success of the Murphy and Co. packinghouse in Des Moines. To attract industries to Des Moines, Allen offered free land to capitalists who would build a starch factory or a reaper and mower factory. Allen's dealings were the subject of much talk; at times it seemed as if he were a living legend. How else to explain the rumor in June 1873 that Allen had cornered the wheat market on the Chicago Board of Trade? The rumor turned out to be false. It was true, however, that Allen speculated heavily in grain. He financed W.N. Sturgis, a board of trade member described in one lawsuit as ''a reckless, daring, and irresponsible speculator.'' Sturgis, using Allen's money, reportedly bought options on twenty million bushels of corn during the summer of 1874. But any alleged control of the market appeared not to benefit Allen, who testified he lost more than $150,000 in the frenetic activity.

Better documented than Allen's commodities speculations were his sprees of landbuying. Robert Swierenga found that Allen was a major buyer of land put on the auction block because taxes were delinquent. These tax purchases were in addition to Allen's previously mentioned acquisition of government lands. Allen was not unusual in that respect; research by Swierenga showed that many prominent tax buyers ''cut their eye teeth on public land speculation and moneylending in connection with it'' before frequenting tax auctions. Allen stood out, though, as one of the largest buyers of all. But Allen's buying of tax-delinquent land did not mean he was taking property from little people. Swierenga found that tax buyers such as Allen were not simply greedy speculators. Rather, Swierenga argued, tax auctions brought funds to local governments unable to borrow in the credit markets. Many bidders were not planning to make a fortune from the land itself, but from the penalty and interest charges paid by delinquent landowners in order to regain their property. The charges were above the rates on standard loans.

The legendary nature of Allen's landholdings was bolstered by accounts such as the one in the February 1874 issue of the *Land Owner,* a Chicago publication. It said, ''From 1855, Allen came prominently before the people of Iowa and his name became a household word in the most remote corner of the commonwealth. It is entirely proper to say that no man was ever so thoroughly, intimately, and favorably known in any community as B.F. Allen has been in Iowa for twenty years. He was a member of the Senate of that state for four years, and inaugurated many reforms in the state government. He has more deeds on record in Iowa than any other man, and it is a significant fact that no mortgage was ever recorded against him in that state. He owns a vast amount of land and a large number of growing townsites throughout the center of the state, which properties are daily enhancing in value as this great commonwealth progresses toward its ultimate destiny. Mr. Allen erected a few years since at the Iowa capital one of the most elegant and costly private residences in the country, rivaling even the Hudson River villas of the Eastern capitalists.'' By the time the article appeared, Terrace Hill, although still owned by Allen, was no longer his primary residence. One year later, even his ownership would be in doubt. The semi-abandonment of the mansion began in May 1873 when Allen obtained controlling interest in Chicago's Cook County National Bank. At the time, the purchase seemed like just one more logical expansion of the Allen empire. But in fact it was an act of great desperation, an attempt to avoid bankruptcy.

The reason that Allen wanted the Cook County National Bank was so that he could ''rob'' it—that is, drain its deposits to pay off the Mississippi and Missouri Railroad bonds that the court was calling in. Allen bought the bank on May 29, 1873, when he obtained 2,665 shares of stock from D.D. Spencer, who was then president. The bank had been formed less than two years earlier, but was already the tenth largest of twenty-one national banks in Chicago. At the beginning of 1873 it had deposits of $880,000 and a capital and surplus account of $505,000. The U.S. Supreme Court told in retrospect how Allen had paid for the bank's stock—in part by writing a check on his New York City bank, and in part by checks drawn on the Chicago bank itself! Although the bank purchase helped Allen make the railroad bond payments, he still needed lots of money to repay other sources. His banks were in debt to one another for large sums, which meant in effect that Allen was using depositors' money in less than ethical ways.

Allen's speculations were going sour. As the U.S. Supreme Court put it, ''It is true that so inveterate a speculator sometimes made a fortunate venture, but his losses were greatly in excess of his gains.'' One venture involved a $400,000 loan by Allen, Stephens and Co. to two men, with the collateral being the Mono Silver Mine in the territory of Utah. The mine proved to be worthless. The bankers were left with a huge deficit, exceeding all the profits they had made in their two years of business. The bank was insolvent, although the public did not know it. Allen's failure to make a profit on his grain dealings hurt, too, especially because his failure was so visible. Excess corn was stored at Rock Island Railroad stations in Iowa, causing no end of comment by train travelers who had never seen anything like it.

It looked as if the end for Allen might come in September 1873, when the Cook County National Bank closed. But the closing turned out to be only temporary. It did not arouse suspicion about the bank's soundness because it came as part of the general monetary collapse precipitated by the troubles of nationally known financier Jay Cooke. In fact, the closing of Allen's bank seemed to enhance his reputation, as he was able to reopen his bank's doors before other banks could open theirs. The *Daily State Register* praised Allen's conduct during the panic. The *Register* recalled the upright performance of a much younger Allen during the panic of 1857, when his Nebraska bank redeemed its paper with gold. ''The financial sagacity that guided Mr. Allen through the panic has attended him ever since,'' the *Register* said. ''His prosperity, as a natural consequence, is continually increasing. . . . Our Des Moines banker has fairly won the distinction he is now gaining, and in this none finds so much pleasure as his everyday neighbors here at his home who know the man so well and know how wholly and unreservedly he is to be trusted.''

That trust was to be short-lived, although there were many people who even after the Chicago bank failed did not see Allen had run it into the ground himself. Instead, he was portrayed as an innocent dupe. Typical was the account of a historian who wrote that ''some evil genius induced Allen to go to Chicago. To become a Napoleon of finance was an honorable ambition. Then, unconscionable bank sharks unloaded on him the Cook County National Bank. He at once applied all his skill and means to bring it to the front, but soon discovered it to be a sepulchre of rottenness. He dumped into it all the resources he could command, and draining day by day the receipts of the bank in Des Moines. It was like pouring water into a rathole. It had no bottom, and it collapsed.'' Such defenders did not realize how ludicrous their argument was. If they were to be believed, Allen was not a crook, but was a fool. They did not attempt to square such stupidity by Allen with their accounts of his sagacity. A devastating refutation of Allen's defenders came from D.D. Spencer, who had sold the Cook County bank to Allen. Spencer noted that at the time of the purchase, Allen had twenty years of experience as a banker, and was worth millions of dollars. ''All the books and records of the Cook County bank were open to his examination,'' Spencer said. ''He considered the condition so good that he not only paid par for the shares he bought, but 10 percent besides. Is it to be supposed that a banker of his experience, shrewdness, and success could have been induced to pay such a sum for worthless property?''

Chapter Five

The Prairie Palace in Limbo

While Allen was trying to save his financial empire from collapse, Terrace Hill, his "prairie palace of the West," suffered dearly. In April 1873, Arathusa and daughter Kitty left the mansion to go on a grand tour of Europe. They would be gone for half a year. Allen himself was spending a lot of time away from Des Moines even before his wife left for Europe. While she was gone, he bought the Chicago bank—apparently without her knowledge—which kept him away from Des Moines more than ever. With Benjamin and Arathusa both gone, Arathusa's parents helped the servants care for Terrace Hill and the younger children. When Arathusa and Kitty returned from Europe, Benjamin was already settled in Chicago, in a suite of rooms at the Grand Pacific Hotel. Arathusa decided to keep the family together at all costs, so within a short time everyone was ensconced in the Chicago hotel with the patriarch. Mrs. West was put in charge of airing out Terrace Hill from time to time, so that it would not become musty. Peter Lambert, the veteran horticulturist, took care of the greenhouse. He sold flowers to the public, keeping some profits for himself and sending the remainder of the money to the Allens in Chicago. A gardener named Strombeck occupied the basement

Grand Pacific Hotel, designed by W. W. Boyington. It looked like this until 1895. (Courtesy Chicago Historical Society.)

of the mansion with his family during the winter of 1873-74. A man named Wilson took care of routine maintenance at Terrace Hill. He also cared for the stable, the stock, and the deer which roamed the grounds. A farm owned by Allen on the east side of Des Moines was maintained by hired hands.

By mid-1874, the Allens had moved out of the Grand Pacific Hotel and into a Chicago house at 988 Prairie Avenue. The cost of the house was $52,500. Much of the expensive furniture from Terrace Hill was shipped to Chicago for use in the house. But because the Chicago residence had not been built on the scale of Terrace Hill, mirrors and carpets had to be cut down to fit. Arathusa later expressed unhappiness that her possessions had been altered for the Prairie Avenue dwelling. "It was a house that never suited me, a house I would never have gone into as a permanent home, and I regretted that I had moved my furniture there," she said. The Allens became legal residents of Chicago. B.F. cast a ballot in city elections there on November 3, 1874. So the question became, "What to do with Terrace Hill?" Arathusa wanted to return there, where she felt the family belonged. But B.F. knew he could not afford to maintain it and a Chicago home, too. The *Daily State Register* of March 22, 1874, reported alternatives being discussed: "Ever since Hon. B.F. Allen removed to Chicago, there has been considerable speculation as to the final disposition of his Des Moines residence, Terrace Hill. It is too extensive for any private fortune of any ordinary dimensions to keep up. Nothing less than the income of a millionaire could occupy it. The Catholic Society has talked of purchasing the property for a school or nunnery, but the affair never amounted to anything but talk." One prospect that appeared favorable was establishing Allen University at Terrace Hill, making Des Moines the site of a top school. The plan was being pushed by Judge C.C. Cole, who went to Chicago in December 1873 to discuss the details with Allen. Cole convinced Allen with little difficulty. In addition to the mansion, there were other buildings on the property that could have been used for the proposed university. They included a "large two-story dwelling suitable for the president's house," brick carriage houses, a brick barn, and several more "capable of being converted at a mere nominal expense into chapels, recitation rooms or to any other desired use," according to one report.

The *Register* said the landscaped grounds would make the site comparable to Cornell University in New York State, and added that the proposed school would surpass anything the State University of Iowa could offer in the way of physical facilities. According to the Allen-Cole agreement, Terrace Hill would be purchased by the Presbyterian Church for $250,000, with Allen contributing $150,000 of the total if several conditions were met. First, he would insist that the institution be named after him. Second, it must have colleges of all the arts, one of science, and others of law, medicine, and theology. Third, it would be open to men and women students on equal terms. Fourth, the church would have to pay its $100,000 share, with interest, to Allen by January 1, 1875. If the conditions were met, Allen would sweeten his already generous offer by endowing the president's chair with $30,000. There was support for the proposal throughout Iowa. Some people believed that classes could open for the September 1874 term. Cole was on the trail of contributions other than Allen's. He was corresponding with trustees of the Parson Fund for endowed professorships. The *Register* reported that an endowment for the college of law was "almost certain from a gentleman of large wealth and noted regard for learning."

Proponents of the university pressured the Presbyterians to act rapidly. The *Register* editorialized: "As Judge Cole expresses the idea, it is to be a liberal university where the broadest range of study can be pursued and the freest thought encouraged. (Allen was insisting that the university be nonsectarian, although it would be under the church's control.) With such a magnificent opportunity, the Presbyterians of Iowa surely cannot and will not permit the opportunity to pass by unimproved. No other church in the state is so well fitted to accept and improve such a princely gift. No other church is so wealthy."

The city of Des Moines was also called upon to help with Allen University. The *Register* said: "The duty of Des Moines in this matter is plain. Mr. Allen proposes to establish here an institution which would be a constant and constantly increasing source of revenue to the city. What Yale College is to the city where it is located, and what Michigan University is to Ann Arbor, Allen University would be to Des Moines. Aside from the expenditures of students, it would attract settlers anxious to locate where their children could enjoy the benefits of a liberal education." Supporters of Allen University noted that earlier plans to bring a university to Des Moines had failed—Parsons College and Des Moines College were examples—but that this plan seemed surer of success, being more than half-accomplished. This plan, however, was to fail, too. In October 1874 Cole got his chance to present the proposal to the Presbyterian Synod. But to his dismay the membership showed little enthusiasm. A committee finally was appointed to consider the matter, and there it eventually died.

So, as 1875 arrived, Allen was still the owner of Terrace Hill. He wanted to sell it, despite his pride in it, because he needed money. His desperation was so great that in November 1874 the mansion became part of a secret agreement between Allen and his New York banking partners. The agreement, known later as the "blanket mortgage," gave Allen $465,476 immediately, with more to come, in exchange for a mortgage on all his real estate. The mortgage was extraordinary in scope, covering rural land in twenty-four Iowa counties and town lots in fourteen Iowa cities. The agreement also covered land owned by Allen in Colorado, Kentucky, and Nebraska. On the basis of those landholdings, Allen eventually borrowed $900,000 from his New York bank. All that time, the mortgage agreement had not been filed for the public to see, as

it should have been by law. Finally in January 1875, about two months after the agreement, the boom fell on Allen. The Cook County National Bank closed permanently and he was forced into bankruptcy court within a month. As his seemingly countless creditors fought over whatever assets Allen had left, the blanket mortgage was discovered. The creditors were outraged, and cried "fraud." Terrace Hill became a key issue in the bankruptcy proceedings, as Stephens and Blennerhassett, the holders of the mortgage, vied with other creditors for possession of the mansion.

Allen realized the house would be the subject of fights among his creditors. However, he had plans to keep it for himself as a symbol of his glory days, even if he were to lose all else. It was a change of heart, considering how he had been working so mightily to sell it before the bankruptcy proceeding. Before the bankruptcy, whatever money Allen received from the sale of the mansion would have gone to him. After the bankruptcy papers were filed, any money realized on Terrace Hill would have gone not to Allen, but to his creditors. As a result, his incentive to sell was lessened, and he began calculating how to retain the mansion. Allen thought he had found the answer in the Iowa bankruptcy law, which allowed a debtor to keep his homestead, no matter what its value. (By comparison, Illinois law at that time limited the value of a homestead to $1,000, the price of the drawing room fireplace mantel in Terrace Hill.)

The Iowa law also allowed Allen up to forty acres, so he marked off the homesite and some of the surrounding land. Even the liberal allowance meant Allen had to surrender much of the Terrace Hill estate, which consisted of sixty-five acres north of the railroad tracks and sixty-nine acres south of the tracks, for a total of 134 acres. It was not such a sacrifice, however, because Allen had intended to sell the southern tract anyway. Allen did everything he could to bolster his case for keeping Terrace Hill under the homestead exemption, anticipating that the creditors would try to negate his claim by saying that Allen had become a resident of Chicago and therefore had no right to a homestead under Iowa statutes. The first move Allen made to bolster his case was to return to Terrace Hill from Chicago on February 1, 1875, about two weeks after the Chicago bank failed, but three weeks before his creditors filed the bankruptcy petition. The children remained in Chicago temporarily, being forbidden to travel because they had contracted the measles. The Prairie Avenue residence was left in the possession of H.L. Swords, the fiance of Kitty Allen. Most of the original Terrace Hill furniture remained in Chicago. To make the mansion livable, the Allens rented furniture from Des Moines dealer Louis Harbach, who had helped to furnish Terrace Hill in 1868. Only the first floor was to be used, for economy's sake—before hard times set in, the Allens had lived on all three floors. At least five of the forty acres were put under cultivation so that the family could grow some of its own food.

Allen's creditors tried to take possession of the mansion's

original furniture, but a judge ruled that it was owned by Arathusa in her own name and thus not subject to the bankruptcy proceeding. Terrace Hill itself was not to be retained so easily, however. For eight years, the ownership of the mansion remained in doubt. There were rulings against Allen's right to keep the house and its forty acres, and rulings in his favor. To understand why it was so confusing, it is helpful to know more about the failure of Allen's Chicago bank and the aftermath. A detailed understanding of the controversy will show that although Allen eventually ''won'' the battle for Terrace Hill, in the end he was a loser. The true beneficiary of the mess was Frederick M. Hubbell.

B. F. Allen. (Courtesy Iowa State Historical Department.)

Chapter Six

Bankruptcy

The Cook County National Bank announced its failure on January 19, 1875, by posting this note on its front door:

> I regret to inform the public that this bank has been compelled to suspend business. Promised and expected aid was refused at the last moment. For this reason the shareholders of the bank have decided to go into voluntary liquidation, as provided in such cases by the national currency act. I can assure depositors that no loss can occur to them, their payment being only a question of time.
>
> B.F. Allen

To those who had been reading the bank's statements of condition only casually, the closing was a shock. Just eight days earlier the bank had published a balance sheet that looked sound. As the *Chicago Times* said, "The statement was comparatively the best among all the banks in the city. . . .(It) did more to make people feel a confidence in the concern than any event at any time since its origin. Was this statement a true one? Did it actually set forth the condition of the bank at that time? And if true, how comes it so closely upon the heels of the exuberant and plethoric statement that a confiding public is startled with a complete failure?" The *Times* answered its own questions by stating that figures can lie: "The figures may have exhibited the exact status of the bank at that time, but it was not a healthy status, very like a certain fat man in the sideshow of a circus, whom a mischievous boy pricked with a pin and thus suddenly reduced him to a skeleton. He had been puffed out with wind. All that money may have been in the bank at the time, but it evidently was not there for keeps. That it was a delusion and a snare, though maybe an honest one, is palpable."

To people who had read the bank's statements carefully, the collapse was not a surprise. The *Times* reported that "bankers, capitalists, and wide-awake businessmen generally received the news without any signs of astonishment, simply remarking 'So it has come at last; the wonder is it did not come sooner,' and then returning to their avocations as if nothing had occurred." Part of the reason for their calmness was their belief that although the bank may have failed, Allen had not. A president of a rival bank estimated Allen's wealth at between $7 million and $10 million. When asked how the bank failure would affect Allen personally, the unnamed president replied, "It will

affect him of course to a certain extent, but it will not ruin him. I know the impression prevails that much of Mr. Allen's property is of a shaky kind, but this is a false impression. I had it myself until convinced to the contrary. In my dealings with him, I will tell you honestly, I was astonished to find how much really valuable property he possesses. . . . To the best of my belief, Mr. Allen would enjoy a competency of two million dollars after paying all his debts, and this under a forced sale. But such a sale is hardly among the probabilities, and if Mr. Allen is allowed to manage his own affairs, as he undoubtedly will, he can, if he should conclude to realize on all his property, save a much larger sum."

In Des Moines, where Allen's customers and friends were not so attuned to the inner workings of Chicago banks, the reaction was one of disbelief. When word arrived in Des Moines of the failure, the *Register* reported that "the news was not credited." Yet when it was confirmed, the overwhelming feeling was one of optimism rather than anger. The National State Bank, headed by Allen, carried on business as usual; so did the Capital City Bank, where Allen was also president. B.F. Allen's private bank did close temporarily, but the closing did not lead to a panic among depositors, who were owed a total of $690,657. More than one hundred Des Moines business leaders gathered in a meeting at Hoyt Sherman's office. If there were negative words said about Allen, they were not reported. "All mention of his name called forth friendly expressions and the resolutions so emphatically endorsing him were adopted with vigorous clapping of hands and very decided applause," one newspaper said. "Hardly a man was talked to on the subject yesterday who did not speak with a voice of swelling gratitude of some timely and substantial kindness Mr. Allen sometime rendered him or his family or his friends, and many an eye moistened with a gratitude that the voice did not express." Some of Allen's friends said that they would sell their possessions in exchange for Allen's securities, such was their confidence that he would redeem all obligations in full. W.W. Moore, once a clerk in Allen's general store and then a successful businessman, said he would accept certificates of deposit on Allen's banks in payment of debts or for goods.

Allen himself, still in Chicago, was not saying much right away. But on January 22, three days after the bank failure, he did write a letter to Des Moines newspapers which read: "In this moment of overwhelming cares and anxiety, it is impossible for me to give you the facts about the great mortgage scare (a reference to his November 18, 1874, blanket mortgage with the New York bank) that is working such mischief. I will do so at the earliest possible moment. In the meantime, I will say that when such facts are presented it will appear that the very means by which I sought to rescue the Cook County bank from embarrassment, and which but for bad faith on the part of others would have succeeded, have been used to precipitate its suspension as well as to attempt to destroy my personal credit and my estate. A prudent moderation on the part of all interested in the latter will enable me to save all from the possibility of loss. The record of my past life is all the answer I have to those who assail my integrity. My present time and energies are devoted to those who have caused the mischief. I have no fears for the conclusion.''

Later statements by Allen were more detailed, and followed the same theme—he was not at fault. His first specific statement laid the blame for the bank failure at the feet of former president D.D. Spencer and Allen's New York banking partners Stephens and Blennerhassett. Allen's only hint of contrition was in a sentence saying, ''That there were many things done by me in the emergency in which I was thrown that were not consistent with sound banking, I do not deny.'' But the remainder of what Allen said focused on how everything that he had done was for the good of the depositors. The sincerity of the statement was not found wanting by most Iowans: When Allen returned from Chicago, about 150 people, including top business leaders, met his train at 3 A.M. The return was clearly a popular move. The next day, in his office at the B.F. Allen Bank, Allen ''was thronged with the people of Des Moines and of surrounding towns, all of them anxious not to inquire about their deposits, but to assure Mr. Allen of their continued confidence in him and his financial solvency,'' according to a newspaper account.

There were some citizens who did not share in the sympathy for Allen, but those speaking unkind words were labeled outside villains by the local press. One newspaper editorialized, ''Mostly they represent either that brutal greed of money which would feed even on human life and human souls, or that malevolence of small souls which lacking the courage to strike when to strike might have been manly and fair, would strike with coward hand now. It is grateful to know that nearly all of this little measure of pitiful enmity is bred and nurtured by outside influences, mainly by the same brutal pack at Chicago.'' The *Register,* probably the most influential of Iowa newspapers, was blind in its support of Allen, who was after all its financial angel. The *Register* almost surely understated the anger directed at Allen in those first weeks. The *Des Moines Daily Journal* raised the hard questions that the more influential *Register* did not ask, and as it turned out, the *Journal* was far more prescient. One of the *Journal's* first dispatches from Chicago after the bank collapse implied that Allen was less than pure. It read in part, ''The affairs of the Cook County National Bank here reached a climax, and it is found to be in utter ruin. Depositors have grown clamorous and a receiver will probably be appointed at an early day. Secret meetings of the stockholders are being held daily. . . . If there are any assets with which to pay dividends, they seem to have so far eluded discovery. The capital of the bank, there is good ground for saying, has been wasted, and all the good papers it held have been pledged in New York for advances.'' In Chicago, the support for Allen in the hinterlands of Des Moines did not impress many people. The *Journal's* Chicago correspondent

wrote that such support was ''so plainly by people whom Allen owns body and soul that it has created more distrust than ever in him, and is looked upon as dictated by him only to cover up his bankrupt condition and gain time.''

The *Journal* said it would withhold judgment until Allen issued a definitive statement, but by January 28, nine days after the failure, the *Journal* editor was withholding judgment no longer. He found Allen's only statements up until then disappointing. One statement was termed ''cunningly worded,'' doing everything but addressing the vital point: Where had the hundreds of thousands of dollars entrusted to Allen gone? The *Journal* did not believe that Allen was guiltless. After asking many specific questions in its columns, the *Journal* stated: ''We think Allen is under some little obligation to those who have fed and clothed him for twenty years, and we still believe that those who have given him their all that he might speculate in grain, luxuriate in grain corners, and dabble in railroad stocks have a few rights that even the once mighty B.F. Allen ought to respect. . . . Mr. Allen (says) that all of his property and energies stand pledged for the benefit of all his creditors. How much will there be left, Mr. Allen, after all the mortgages you have given during the past three months are satisfied?'' Some observers went even further, charging out-and-out illegal practices by Allen. The *Chicago Tribune,* after looking into the failure for several months, charged that Allen ''repeatedly violated the provisions of the law relating to the power of a national bank to lend money.''

There was enough substance to the charges of illegalities that later Allen was tried two times over the failure of the Cook County bank. In April 1877 Allen was indicted by a Chicago grand jury for embezzlement and other alleged crimes. He was charged individually on eleven counts and jointly with bank clerk Arnold M. Cleveland on six additional counts. One of the counts said that Allen in January 1875 converted $500,000 of depositors' money to his personal use. The indictments were of such interest that the *New York Times* ran the story on its front page. Eventually the indictments were split into two categories, and brought to trial separately in 1880. At the first trial, Allen was acquitted of the embezzlement charges. At the second trial, he was acquitted of charges that he made false reports to federal agencies. The jury deliberated only ten minutes. Those trials were in the future, however—in January 1875, Allen's creditors were not thinking so much of retribution as they were wondering if they would see their money again, as Allen was promising.

The creditors were to learn that Allen's promises were mostly empty ones. That is why on February 23, 1875, they pushed Allen into bankruptcy. The move came after a meeting of the creditors with Allen's lawyer at Moore's Opera House in Des Moines on February 5. Depending on which newspaper account one believed, there were either 250, 300, or 500 creditors in attendance. Attorney C.H. Gatch presented a balance sheet that showed Allen's assets topping his liabilities by $837,828. The creditors were dubious, however—with good reason, as it turned out. By April 5, Allen was saying that his liabilities had increased due to a variety of circumstances. He asked his creditors to drop bankruptcy proceedings in exchange for payment of twenty-five cents on the dollar, in three annual installments. The creditors, who a couple of months earlier were told they would get their money back dollar for dollar, did not take kindly to the offer. On April 22, 1875, Allen was officially adjudged a bankrupt. The question then became, who would handle the complex estate so that creditors would regain as much money as possible? The choice was Hoyt Sherman. Thus began Sherman's nine-year task as assignee in bankruptcy, sorting out who was to get what.

One of the most troublesome assets from the beginning was Terrace Hill. After Sherman's appointment, Terrace Hill was

Hoyt Sherman. (Courtesy Iowa State Historical Department.)

conveyed to him by Allen in a deed filed July 16 with the Polk County recorder. Allen conveyed the deed under legal duress —he continued to claim the mansion as rightfully his under the homestead exemption in Iowa's bankruptcy law. The creditors claimed the mansion as theirs, though, contending that Allen's true homestead was in Chicago. During the uncertainty, the Allen family continued to live in the mansion, although B.F. and Arathusa were often absent. For instance, in the summer of 1875 they traveled to Utah, ostensibly because of Arathusa's health. On December 7, 1875, Kitty Allen was married at Terrace Hill. The *Register* termed the mansion the "family residence" in its account of the wedding, an indication that many persons still considered it to be the home of the Allens, notwithstanding the pending legal questions. Despite Allen's shaky finances, the wedding turned out to be posh. "The family of the bride had intended making the occasion a very quiet affair, celebrating the happy event without the least ostentation," said one account. "But the large circle of friends of the groom at Chicago and in the East and South sent a large deputation of their number with the colonel to attend the nuptials, and they, representing a great deal of wealth and all coming from very fashionable society, made the wedding quite a brilliant affair after all." The "colonel" whom the eldest Allen child was marrying was H.L. Swords of Chicago. He had fought with the Union army in the Civil War. After that he settled in New Orleans where he was active in Louisiana politics. In Chicago he was a successful businessman. So, for a night at least, Terrace Hill regained some of the splendor that had permeated it at the housewarming seven years before. How things had changed since then!

The display of wealth at the wedding did not seem to cause resentment among the Des Moines creditors of Allen, who were still waiting for their money. Gifts from Des Moines residents were presented to Kitty. One guest was Hoyt Sherman, the very man whose job it was to take Terrace Hill away from the Allens. (Sherman and Allen apparently remained friends throughout the trying bankruptcy proceedings. One indication was the name Sherman gave to a son—Frank Allen Sherman.) The scope of Sherman's job as assignee was mind-boggling. The bankruptcy docket showed 218 creditors filing claims the first day the docket opened. Sherman had to investigate the validity of each claim. Hundreds more were filed later. In June 1875, Allen provided Sherman with what was supposed to be a complete rundown of indebtedness. That list—which turned out to be incomplete—contained 560 creditors. The amount owed was about $2 million. The total was much larger if hundreds of thousands of dollars in claims by Stephens and Blennerhassett were figured in.

The first sale of Allen's property occurred August 14, 1875. On the auction block were ten horses, one colt, one piano, two organs, and stock in the Des Moines Water Works. Sherman settled some claims with creditors amicably, but often the parties could not agree on what was fair. In those instances, U.S.

District Judge James M. Love had to decide each claim on its merit. The decisions were as wide-ranging as the claims themselves. For instance:

• More than 300 lots in Des Moines were divided between Allen's estate and Des Moines lawyer George W. Clark, a partner of Allen's. Those lots constituted a large portion of what was then the city of Des Moines.

• A dispute with Hawkeye Insurance Co., which Allen had helped to found, was settled when Allen agreed to turn back 250 shares of stock. In return, Hawkeye dropped claims against Allen in his role as company treasurer totaling $30,000. The agreement avoided a potentially messy battle, one that might have involved allegations of embezzlement.

• Allen's landholdings in numerous Iowa counties were sold by Sherman to raise money for the reimbursement of creditors. The counties included Polk, Carroll, Greene, Madison, Guthrie, Warren, Cass, and Pottawattamie, an indication of the scope of Allen's empire. Purchasers of the land had to pay one-fourth or more of the sales price in cash, with the balance due in eighteen months at 7 percent interest.

Within the limitations imposed by the bankruptcy proceedings, Allen cut his own deals, hoping to salvage what he could for himself. In the spring of 1875 Allen attempted to transfer at least 3,500 acres of land he owned in six counties to Chauncey T. Bowen, a banking associate, for $100,000. But the title to the land was clouded by the questionable blanket mortgage given the previous year to Allen, Stephens and Co. It was difficult, as a result, for Bowen to be certain that the land was his. The clouded titles on other pieces of property bedeviled

Savery House. (Courtesy Paul K. Ashby.)

Allen in his efforts to find buyers. Allen used funds he still controlled to buy additional shares of stock in a land company he had formed seven years earlier with John Cook and Ebenezer Cook. The purpose was to obtain property along the route of the Rock Island Railroad. The three men had close ties to the railroad management, which presumably gave them advance knowledge of what new routes would be. According to court records, in 1875 Allen acquired the Cooks' interests in the company from heirs of John and Ebenezer. Rock Island Railroad officials, however, challenged Allen's ownership claims. Thousands of parcels of land were involved: Allen contended he owned almost entire towns along the railroad route west of Des Moines, such as Stuart in Guthrie County and Atlantic in Cass County. Eventually the court awarded a portion of the lands to Allen's estate, and a portion to Rock Island officials.

As the bankruptcy case dragged on from one year to the next, there were many repercussions. Des Moines banks with which Allen had been associated changed hands. At least one eventually failed. That was the National State Bank.

The bankruptcy of Allen also led to the closing of the Savery House in Des Moines, one of the state's best-known hotels. There had been a $40,000 mortgage on the building, with Allen as one of the people granting the mortgage. But unbeknownst to many, Allen had included the Savery House in a collateral package to obtain a $200,000 loan from the Newark, New Jersey, Savings Bank. The bank foreclosed on the mortgage, and in November 1878 halted operation of the hotel. Shortly after the hotel closed, Allen and proprietor James Savery traveled to Montana together, possibly to escape their creditors for awhile.

Governments as well as private enterprises suffered because of Allen's fall. A typical example involved Adair County, Iowa. Because there were no banks within the county, the treasurer deposited tax receipts in B.F. Allen's Des Moines bank. At the time of the bankruptcy, the county had $5,000 on deposit. None of the money was recovered. When Allen was discharged from bankruptcy in December 1875 (meaning that he could get a fresh start, even though his creditors were waiting for payment), there was still much goodwill toward him. One newspaper account was optimistic about the future of Allen, only forty-six years of age: ''Mr. Allen is still a young man with vast capabilities and all of his old-time energies. With his knowledge of business and the confidence that the public still has in his integrity and in his determination to right his fallen fortunes and pay his debts, he will speedily get upon his feet and into a position where he can more rapidly and certainly do justice to his creditors.''

It was not to turn out that way, however. The creditors did not see any money as the months passed, turning into years. Terrace Hill, looming over the city, was a constant reminder of the money Allen once had. Whatever was left was tied up in litigation. A July 1877 report by Hoyt Sherman noted 300 lawsuits related to the bankruptcy. Some creditors began to wonder if the delay was a conspiracy involving Sherman and Allen. Creditor James C. Gibbs asked in a letter to newspapers why things were not moving more quickly. ''It seems to me,'' Gibbs wrote, ''that the creditors of B.F. Allen have waited patiently and a long time, and without discourtesy or doubts of the integrity of any person. I believe the time has come when the creditors should employ a competent accountant and go over the whole and learn just how the business stands.'' There was no doubt that Sherman, however pure his intentions, benefited financially from a prolonged bankruptcy proceeding. He received not only his fees allowed by law, but also extra sums awarded by the court due to the complexity of the case. In 1883, after numerous creditor complaints, a judge was appointed to investigate Sherman's conduct as assignee. Sherman was cleared after a five-month inquiry. Lots of lawyers were benefiting from the case, for that matter. The firm of Polk and Hubbell often represented Sherman in court, making money on each appearance.

While the bankruptcy dragged on, Allen suffered non-financial setbacks that kept him from getting back on his feet. The worst was the death of Arathusa on January 30, 1877, in Chicago. She had been ill for awhile. The causes were unknown, although some observers attributed it to the monetary misfortunes that had befallen the family. Des Moines lawyer Nourse in his memoirs wrote that Arathusa ''had become insane and imagined that her husband's creditors were pursuing her because of their losses. She died within a few months after losing her reason.'' Allen was left with three children at home—Frank, thirteen; Bessie, ten; and Harry, seven. Arathusa was a popular woman, and her death at age forty shocked many citizens. One obituary said: ''Everywhere the news was received with the greatest sorrow. For here for long years, through childhood and through womanhood, Mrs. Allen had been known as scarcely any other woman in Des Moines had been known, and this news touched her back again with all of the old-time tenderness into the hearts and affections of everyone. . . .The good heart which always her life through filled her breast won the love of all who knew her when she was the modest, winsome, cordial, and unaffected girl of a village, the light, life, and pride of a settlement on the frontier. The virtues of her girlhood—her affability, her good-heartedness, her thorough plebianism in claiming friends regardless of rank or condition, and her hearty way of judging people by hearts and not by tinsel—changed with her years only to grow more positive and pronounced.''

The obituary noted ''the noble manner in which she bore the extreme reverses of fortune which came to her in the misfortunes of her husband. She never cared as to the effect upon herself or her family. The only thing with her that grew from brooding thought into morbid ill was that others suffered more than she suffered, and suffered beyond her power to mend. The grief of loss of money, or of the loss of anything which it ever brings in its train, never wore upon her health nor cankered in her heart. The harm that came to her health, if any came in that way, was from the words inflicted upon her by the invasion of her house and family by one or two almost satanic newspapers which always seemed to delight and never to tire in striking even at the wife and children of Mr. Allen—and in wounding her as a true woman is always the soonest and most easily wounded: through the heart. How much this torturing and ingenious unkindness wore away of the life completing its course yesterday we of this world may not know.''

Part of the obituary was devoted to the downtrodden B.F. Allen. The newspaper said: ''To Mr. Allen, trouble has come fairly like an epidemic. Life has shattered almost utterly in his grasp. And calamities have come only to increase in magnitude. Cut down from the high estate of princely fortune and almost princely rank and falling—whether from his own faults or by the inexorable die of fate, we will not stop here beside a grave to discuss—from the proudest places to the lowliest, there was yet in store for him the greater losses which since have come, till now there is in no breast a heart which does not pity the man in his overwhelming sorrows, and feel and express a brother's compassion for him in his woe. And as he shall come to his old home with his dead wife and his little children orphaned of mother to bury in the earth of Des Moines the idolized one whose death has broken up his house, we are sure there are in all the city none who will not feel in their own hearts something of the sorrow he feels, nor any who will not deeply sympathize with a man on whom has fallen a series of calamities which have grown harsher and more cruel at every change.''

It would be easy to write hundreds more pages about the Allen bankruptcy until its disposition, but that will have to be the province of some other history. This book will examine the two key issues holding up settlement of the Allen estate. One was the validity of the November 18, 1874, blanket mortgage on his property that Allen gave to his New York City bank. The mortgage eventually passed to the Charter Oak Life Insurance Co., so the battle became one between the life insurer and Sherman (on behalf of Allen's creditors) over who would receive whatever money the sale of Allen's holdings would bring. The second key issue was who was entitled to Terrace Hill itself—Allen, or his creditors? After numerous attempts at compromise failed, each issue was ruled upon by the federal courts. The decisions provide insight into why Terrace Hill finally passed to F.M. Hubbell.

On May 22, 1878, the trial court issued its decision in the blanket mortgage case. The mortgage was declared void, which meant that if the court ruling were upheld on appeal, Allen's creditors would receive the proceeds from the sale of Allen's property. In the decision, the judge had some uncomplimentary remarks to make about the parties involved. He called Allen, Stephens, and Blennerhassett men whose word could not be trusted, even under oath. "The parties to this mortgage have given much conflicting evidence," the judge said. "Indeed, it seems to be a law of nature with them to contradict one another. Whatever Allen affirms, Stephens and Blennerhassett deny, and whatever Stephens and Blennerhassett affirm, Allen directly controverts. We shall spend no time in the vain effort to sift, weigh, and reconcile their testimony. It must be obvious to anyone who has given careful attention to the record in this case that no court could safely place its judgment upon the testimony of these witnesses. Their disregard of truth and of moral obligations is so apparent that except where they happen to be corroborated, we cannot rely on their testimony." The Charter Oak company of course did not like the blanket mortgage outcome, and appealed all the way to the Supreme Court of the United States, but lost. Sherman later estimated he spent $60,000 from the bankruptcy estate to fight the blanket mortgage claim. And in the end, Charter Oak Life got a bundle of money anyway, as courts upheld the company's claims against Allen as a partner in Allen, Stephens and Co., as opposed to Allen the individual. That later award to Charter Oak topped $700,000.

The disposition of the other key issue—the Terrace Hill case—was not as significant financially for Allen's creditors, but it was vital to the future of the mansion. A trial court decision of 1878 said that Allen was not entitled to keep Terrace Hill under the homestead exemption in Iowa's bankruptcy law. The case turned on the question of whether Allen had been sincere when he told Des Moines residents in 1873 that he would retain the city as his home, despite his extensive holdings in Chicago. The court did not believe Allen. It said: "It is only when men's words and actions coincide that any great importance is to be given to the former. We therefore attach less importance than counsel seem to do to the declarations of Mr. Allen at Des Moines and to citizens of that place. Mr. Allen owned a bank at Des Moines with very large deposits. The evidence shows that it was of vital importance to him to keep up and maintain the deposits of his Des Moines bank. It required no great sagacity to see that the Des Moines bank would be greatly injured by the prevalence of a belief that he had permanently abandoned his residence there."

The court said the evidence showed Allen would have sold his once-beloved mansion if he could have obtained what he thought to be a reasonable price. "The facts lead the mind irresistably to this conclusion," the court said. "The fact that Mr. Allen purchased a controlling interest in a great bank in Chicago, became its president, and took personal direction of its affairs; that he purchased a house in Chicago at a cost of (over) $50,000, stripped his Des Moines house of its expensive furniture to furnish it, and cut down costly mirrors and carpets taken from his Iowa house to adapt them to his new home; that simultaneously with the purchase of the Chicago house he offered his Iowa homestead for sale and actually entered into a contract for the sale. . . . These facts, we say, form a chain of

evidence utterly inconsistent with the hypothesis that Mr. Allen did not intend to abandon his domicile in Iowa and fix his permanent residence in Illinois."

Despite the authoritative-sounding court ruling, the matter did not end there. Allen succeeded in having the matter reopened. In May 1883, to the surprise of many observers, Allen reached an agreement with Hoyt Sherman that gave Allen ownership of Terrace Hill. Why Sherman agreed to the settlement and why a judge approved it in light of the earlier ruling is not known. One newspaper account hinted at new evidence on Allen's behalf, but was not more specific. Allen retained the mansion and about eight acres. Sherman received about thirty-two acres on behalf of Allen's creditors. The ground to the west of the house that Sherman won was to be laid out into lots for homes and placed on the market. At Sherman's insistence the settlement included provisions for an avenue eighty feet wide along the west line of the land retained by Allen.

After the two key issues were resolved, the Allen bankruptcy was settled expeditiously. Sherman's role as assignee officially ended on October 30, 1884. Most creditors received some money, but not much. Nourse put the amount at fifteen cents on the dollar. Many of the assets Allen had remaining had been bought by F.M. Hubbell and J.S. Polk for about ten cents on the dollar. A tabulation in Hubbell's diaries for 1883 showed the claims against Allen's estate to be about $4 million. Hubbell and Polk acquired at least $3.3 million of that by paying $350,000. They would not have spent that sum, of course, unless they believed there was a profit to be realized. Hubbell's biographer George Mills wrote, "How Hubbell and Polk came out on the venture is not set down in (Hubbell's) diary. They had the money to hold on to the property, however. And times improved. There is every reason to believe that they earned a good profit on the Allen assets."

Hubbell's personal coup involved Terrace Hill. Most important to Hubbell, he obtained the mansion in his own name. Together with Polk, he had obtained thirty-two acres of the grounds from Sherman. But the transaction for the house itself was made directly with its builder. The deed transferring the mansion to Frances and F.M. Hubbell was dated May 9, 1884. The amount paid was $60,000, less than one-fourth of what it had cost Allen to build and furnish the house only seventeen years earlier. The sale of the residence was noticed far and wide. The *Iowa State Register* said on May 10: "One of the most notable homesteads in the city or state was sold yesterday afternoon, the transfer being made by a Des Moines man to a Des Moines man. The house was originally surrounded by forty acres of as fine land as was near the city. The place was known as Terrace Hill. For years the settlement of the estate has kept matters in such shape that the place has not been kept up as it used to be . . . . It has not been generally known that the property was for sale. Yesterday afternoon Mr. F.M. Hubbell bought the homestead . . . . The price paid was

B. F. Allen's home—taken from a stereoptican card. (Courtesy Iowa State Historical Department.)

$60,000, and the sale was made in a very short time. Mr. Hubbell bought it for a home and will soon become a resident of the already fashionable avenue. It is one of the most notable transfers of real estate which has ever been made in this city.''

The Hubbell and Polk purchase of the thirty-two acres from Sherman was the first step in dividing the land into seventy-four lots and selling them as homesites. The $350,000 paid by the law partners also gave them huge amounts of Polk County real estate other than Terrace Hill property, as well as land outside of Polk County. So ended Allen's role in the fate of Terrace Hill. But even though he was no longer the owner of the mansion, he could not seem to escape its shadow. In fact, Allen lived almost literally within its shadow after Hubbell became the master. What happened to Allen after his downfall is admittedly not vital to this history of Terrace Hill, but it is an interesting saga.

Young Des Moines socialites, including Bessie Allen (believed to be in center front) daughter of Benjamin and Arathusa Allen. (Courtesy Paul K. Ashby.)

Chapter Seven

Allen's Twilight

It would seem that B.F. Allen had been disgraced by his downfall, but not everyone in the Iowa aristocracy saw it that way. During Allen's second trial for bank fraud in 1880, the list of character witnesses included U.S. Sen. William Allison, Des Moines Mayor W.H. Merritt, *Register* editor Ret Clarkson, Des Moines pioneer P.M. Casady, and even Hoyt Sherman, who was still serving as bankruptcy assignee in the Allen case. Yet Allen was down-and-out, at least temporarily. He had exiled himself to Leadville, Colorado. He was so pressed for money that he could not pay his lawyers, and requested that the government pay the expenses of his witnesses.

Allen did not run away from Des Moines, though. That his family was not cast out from society is shown by the guest list of an 1882 sheet and pillowcase masquerade party at the Armory Hall in McCain's Building. Allen's daughter Bessie was present. The former multimillionaire did not live the remainder of his life in penury, either. By 1884, he had cash from the sale of Terrace Hill. The 1885 Census listed Allen as living at 1022 High Street in Des Moines with four children, two grandchildren, a nurse, and a domestic. He had not remarried after his wife's death, and never would. Allen's occupation was given as president of an insurance company. That same year, the magazine *Inland Architect and Builder* published a detailed sketch of a residence that Terrace Hill designer Boyington had done for Allen. The house apparently was intended for construction in Des Moines. The magazine said the cost would be $11,000—small in comparison to what Terrace Hill had cost, but still a hefty amount for that time. The design was probably never used, but Allen did indeed build a similar house in Des Moines, about 1887. And, of all places, he built it immediately to the west of Terrace Hill. Furthermore, it was built on a tract that was part of the Terrace Hill acreage which Polk and Hubbell had bought from the bankruptcy estate. Mortgage records indicated that Allen borrowed money from Hubbell to finance the purchase of the house. The lot was in what had become known as the Polk and Hubbell Park addition to Des Moines. Allen was to retain the property in the shadow of Terrace Hill until 1900, although the house was not inhabited by Allen full-time. For example, county records indicated that in 1892 the house was occupied by a tenant named Robert Fullerton. By then Allen had moved to California. But he returned to Des Moines frequently, and apparently his heart remained in Iowa, even while he was physically elsewhere. A report to the 1894 Pioneer Lawmakers Association reunion in Des Moines related the status of members not attending, including Allen. The report read: "Benjamin F. Allen of Polk County, a member of the Senate in the thirteenth and fourteenth general assemblies, has spent much of his time for the last five years in California, working for Uncle Sam. He still retains his homestead in Des Moines and considers the capital city his home."

There was additional evidence of Allen's feelings for Des Moines in a letter he sent on the occasion of the capital city's fifty-year anniversary, celebrated July 8, 1896. The letter, dated July 11 from San Dimas, California, said: "It is nearly fifty years since I located at the Raccoon Forks and Fort Des Moines. What an eventful period that has been to myself as well as to the city of Des Moines and to the great state of Iowa. One of the saddest things connected with this is to think how few there are now living of those that we had for friends and neighbors in those early days. From the day I landed at Raccoon Forks and Fort Des Moines, I always had great faith in its future greatness and always predicted that Des Moines would grow to be the largest and most important city in the great state of Iowa. You all know that in that, I certainly was not mistaken. I wish I could find words to tell you what my heart would dictate of my recollections of those early days, which I think were the happiest of my life. But I cannot do it. I can only say my heart was with you all on July 8, 1896." When Allen first moved to California, he apparently settled in Tulare County, several hundred miles north of Los Angeles, and inland. By 1892, however, he had moved to Los Angeles County. He lived there the rest of his life, except for his stays in Des Moines. By 1900, when he was seventy-one, Allen must have decided that frequent trips to Des Moines were too wearing. He sold his house in the shadow of Terrace Hill to William F. West of Los Angeles County. West was probably a relative on Arathusa's side of the family. Two years later West sold the house to Allen's daughter Kitty Swords of New York City. The house left the Allen family in 1903 when it was purchased by a Des Moines man for his home.

Not a lot is known of Allen's life in California, but he did well for himself, although never coming close to building the kind of fortune he had acquired before his collapse. One chronicler of Polk County's history, writing in 1898, said Allen had originally moved to California to accept a position as special agent of the U.S. land office, an "onerous" job. The account said that in 1898, Allen was living on a fruit farm he had purchased. Oranges were his most important crop, and oranges got Allen involved in politics once again. A Los Angeles newspaper reported that Allen's "acquaintance with men of affairs and his natural ability for forcing his point won him a chance with the organized orange growers of California when the fight over the tariff on oranges was at its height. They sent him to Washington, where he exercised every effort and finally won his struggle for the tariff.''

Allen died in the Hollywood section of Los Angeles in 1914, two weeks shy of his eighty-fifth birthday. Even in death he was controversial. The obituaries, despite their inaccuracies on a number of factual matters, showed the perceptions of the vastness of Allen's power in decades gone by. An obituary published in the *Annals of Iowa* said Allen ''is credited with doing more toward developing the city of Des Moines in its early history than any other one man.'' When one considers that Allen's competition for that designation included F.M. Hubbell, the statement was quite an honor. Des Moines' leading newspaper at the time, the *Register and Leader,* played the story of Allen's death on page one. It contained so many errors that it is worthless as a historical record. But it showed how Allen had been thought of by using descriptions such as ''one of the foremost financial powers in Iowa and the Middle West'' and relating that ''at one time he owned every other section of land along the Rock Island Railroad from Davenport to Council Bluffs.''

Allen's once great power apparently was known far beyond Iowa. How else to account for the substantial obituary in a Los Angeles newspaper? The four-deck headline said:

Finis.

ONCE RICHEST MAN IN IOWA.

Former Multi-Millionaire Is Dead of Old Age.

Financed Building of Rock Island Through Iowa.

Caught in Early Financial Panic and Crushed.

After Allen's death, his body was shipped to Des Moines where it was buried in Woodland Cemetery along with that of his wife Arathusa and their children Kitty, Bessie, Fannie, and Thusie. However great his power might have been, it did not seem great after death. His grave is marked only by a small plain headstone. Not even the birth and death dates inscribed on it are correct. But Allen has a more substantial memorial, one that was mentioned prominently in every obituary. That memorial can today be seen from Woodland Cemetery by looking south. It is Terrace Hill.

Almost hidden by the grass, B. F. Allen's gravestone in Woodland Cemetery is dated 1827-1912. Actually B.F. Allen was born in 1829 and died in 1914.

Chapter Eight

The Wealthiest Man in Iowa

While B.F. Allen was on his way to losing a vast fortune, F.M. Hubbell was on his way to gaining an even vaster one. The question is, how was Hubbell able to accumulate the wealth that allowed him to buy not only Terrace Hill, but also much of the remainder of Allen's empire? And what was there about Hubbell that differed from Allen, so that Hubbell never made the mistakes that lost him a fortune? The answers are complex, but shorthand versions can be given here. First, the

Frederick Marion Hubbell. (Courtesy Iowa State Historical Department.)

base of Hubbell's empire was the Equitable Life Insurance Co. of Iowa. A more stable base can hardly be imagined. There was some risk in the life insurance business in the early years of a company, when as with any new venture there was the question of attracting enough customers to remain in existence. After that bridge was crossed, however, there was little need for worry. Competently managed life insurance companies rarely lost money. The same is true today. Second, Hubbell bolstered his insurance company investment with something nearly as stable—land. Almost all of his land was within Des Moines where he could watch over it himself. Third, Hubbell had patience. Even when it appeared that his investment acumen had failed—as when railroads he operated lost money year after year—the appearance could be deceiving. Some of those railroads were eventually sold for a large sum. If Hubbell had bailed out early, he would never have seen the money from the later sales. This is not to say that Hubbell snapped his fingers and became the wealthiest man in Iowa history. When Hubbell became the master of Terrace Hill, he was well-established at forty-five years old, his life not even half over. But it took some doing to get to that position. What follows is an in-depth examination of Hubbell's personal and business lives from the formation of the Equitable Life Insurance Co. in 1867 until the acquisition of Terrace Hill in 1884, the same period in which Allen was going under. The remainder of Hubbell's amazing history—which is inseparable from Terrace Hill's history—will be treated in other chapters.

After returning to Des Moines from western Iowa, Hubbell started buying and selling land—lots of it. Polk County records showed that from 1860 to 1875 Hubbell was involved in at least 400 transactions. Some parcels were purchased from Allen. Hubbell bought land from his own father, too, who had fore-seen the value of frontier parcels as early as 1855. That was why the Hubbells journeyed from Connecticut to Des Moines in the first place. Hubbell's younger brother Solon was buying Des Moines land as well, although Frederick may have been behind those purchases. In fact, Frederick was often the notary public who put the seal on Solon's transactions. (According to Hubbell's biographer, Solon did not have the chance to ac-cumulate much land: In 1874 at age twenty-nine Solon re-portedly absconded with $500 from the Equitable Life Insurance Co. treasury. He was believed to have drowned in the Mississippi River near Saint Louis later that year. Solon was the last of Hubbell's siblings; sister Anna died in 1864 at age twenty-one.) By the late 1860s Hubbell had begun to buy Raccoon River lowlands property that he would later develop into a manufacturing-warehousing-railroad district. Today the area is known as the Factory Addition of Des Moines. Often Hubbell would obtain dozens of parcels the same day by bidding at delinquent tax auctions. The study by Robert Swierenga that chronicled Allen's activity at tax sales showed that Hubbell bought 1,600 liens in the 1860s and 1870s in the sixteen counties examined. Polk County was not even among those sixteen.

Hubbell was so busy with his land dealings that he did not have time to devote to other ventures in which he had become involved before the age of thirty. So in 1868 he sold his interest in the Des Moines Street Railway. An even bigger decision was his resignation as an officer of Equitable Life. The resignation removed Hubbell from the company's day-to-day operations, which Hoyt Sherman took over by himself. But Hubbell was not out of the picture. He remained a director and a member of the board's executive committee. He also began buying the stock of some of his fellow company founders. That stock became increasingly valuable as Equitable Life grew to be a major life insurer.

While building his fortune, Hubbell was trying to plant the roots of his personal life. His family grew, but slowly—in that, as in most other things, Hubbell moved with caution. After son Frederick Cooper was born in 1864, F.M. and his wife Frances waited a decade before having a second child. They named her Beulah. The Hubbells' last child was not born for nearly another decade. That was Grover, who arrived the year

before the Hubbells obtained Terrace Hill. While the family was growing, the Hubbells moved quite a bit within Des Moines. Presumably each move was to a better home than the one Hubbell had built in 1865. The 1866 Des Moines city directory showed the Hubbell residence at Fourth and South streets. In 1869, the directory listed the family's address on South between Second and Third streets. Two years later, the Hubbell's address was Chestnut Street between Second and Third, and in 1873 it was listed as the corner of Fifth and Sycamore streets. The family resided there until the move to Terrace Hill, if the directories were accurate. In 1878 Hubbell had a telephone connection installed between his home and his office. It was the first in Des Moines.

Hubbell was never so busy with his personal life or his established businesses that he ignored promising new ventures. In 1871, he was a primary figure in the organization of the Des Moines Water Co. Hubbell served as company secretary for years. Water was taken from chambers excavated under the bed of the Raccoon River. The system was praised as giving Des Moines ''the purest and best water of any city

Grover Cooper Hubbell.

Beulah Cooper Hubbell.

in the union. The city is also provided with an adequate and reliable fire service." Within five years, the water company had built fifteen miles of water mains and was pumping 800,000 gallons a day. Hubbell was intimately involved in company operations. One of his diary entries in 1883 showed him in the field testing water main pressure. Hubbell's involvement, however, had its drawbacks. He was the target of attacks by opponents of the utility, who believed it was in the wrong hands. Some of the attacks were issued by city officials, who attempted to cancel the long-term charter granted in 1871 so that the water company would become municipally owned. Municipal ownership did come, but not until 1919.

Along with his partner Polk, Hubbell was doing so well in so many undertakings that in 1875 the two men announced they were entering the general banking business, with corre-spondents in Chicago and New York to serve their Des Moines operations. The business would be conducted from their exist-ing office on Mulberry Street. The office had been outfitted with "one of the best and most secure vaults in the state," according to a newspaper account, which added that the vault was "supplied with a $1,200 safe, of the latest and best pattern, with locks (that are) burglar and powder proof." One com-mentator welcomed the move by Hubbell and Polk, saying, "They have been associated in business ever since 1861. For several years past they have engaged in the business of brokers. They are gentlemen of ample means and careful business habits, not given to speculation and conservative in all their transactions.

Des Moines Water Works. (Courtesy Paul Ashby.)

They will doubtless find a niche in Des Moines banking that they will fill with profit to themselves and to their customers." Hubbell's energy in new ventures was concentrated in rail-roading, though. He never tried to become a railroad baron like Jay Gould, or even B.F. Allen. Instead, Hubbell invested in Iowa railroads with narrow gauge tracks. He was not sorry about his strategy—although some lines had losses more years than not, they turned out to be valuable properties that the national railroads bought for a pretty penny.

In 1866 the Iowa and Minnesota Railway Co. was organized during a meeting at the Polk County Courthouse. The goal was to construct a line north from Des Moines to Ames and another line south to Indianola. But before the work could be completed in either direction, the company was in financial trouble. It had to be sold. The southern portion of the line was transferred to the already existing Des Moines, Indianola and Missouri Railroad Co. The northern portion from Des Moines to Ames was sold in 1869 to Hubbell and Polk. Hubbell was about to begin his reign as a railroad magnate of sorts. To complete the line, Hubbell decided to ask townships along the proposed route to provide tax subsidies. A number of townships agreed, and $118,000 was accumulated. As Hubbell put it: "It was believed that this amount if offered to the Chicago and Northwestern Railway Co. would be sufficient to induce it to construct its road from Ames to Des Moines. This offer was accordingly made by letter and in person at different times during the years 1871 and 1872, but was as often declined. So, early in 1873 the company determined to wait no longer for outside help, but rather to solicit subscriptions to its stock. When enough had been pledged, construction would be commenced." The subscription was successful enough so that Hubbell and Polk conveyed the necessary property to the company, and on January 12, 1874, Iowa Gov. C.C. Carpenter drove the spike to launch the laying of track. By August, the thirty-seven mile line had been completed at a cost of $300,000. The railroad began operating with four locomotives, three passenger cars, four baggage cars, ten stock cars, eighteen flatcars, and twenty-three boxcars. The name was changed from the Iowa and Minnesota to the Des Moines and Minnesota. In 1879 the Chicago and Northwestern, which seven years earlier had refused a chance to build the line, bought it. The move was popular. One newspaper said: "Des Moines people can well rejoice that this north and south line has fallen into the hands of such excellent management as that which controls the Northwestern. This road is noted as having the finest roadbed, the most elegant equipment, and the most genial and least dictatorial officiary of any railway line running into Chicago. These elements will make it very popular in Des Moines, especially as it comes in the capacity of a strong com-peting company, and gives us all visions ahead of an occasional little railway war, with cheap passenger and freight rates for the time being and reasonable rates at all times."

The sale was not the end of Hubbell's involvement in railroading. Actually, in 1879 his heavy involvement was just beginning. In that year, Hubbell became treasurer of the newly organized Des Moines, Adel and Western Railroad, the successor to an earlier company called the Des Moines, Northern and Western which had been established near the start of the decade in Dallas County. In total trackage, the company had twenty-nine miles, from Adel to Redfield and from Redfield to Panora. Like most Iowa railroads with which Hubbell became involved, the track was narrow gauge, meaning three feet wide instead of the standard four feet, eight and one-half inches. Narrow gauge lines were less expensive to build and to operate, and so became popular during the railroading boom of the early 1880s. Hubbell assumed the presidency of the just formed Narrow Gauge Railway Construction Co. in 1880. The company built some of the lines that Hubbell was later to own. In 1881, one of those lines became a reality. It was called the Saint Louis,

The head in this painting belongs to Frederick Cooper Hubbell. The body of the painting was done first by an itinerant artist.

Des Moines and Northern Railway Co. Hubbell was treasurer of the line that ran forty-two miles from Des Moines to Boone. It cost just over $1 million to build. Hubbell apparently owned about $200,000 worth of stock at the beginning. Operation of the railroad was not always profitable, according to annual reports of the Iowa Board of Railroad Commissioners. After two years of operation, the Saint Louis, Des Moines and Northern had a $24,000 deficit. About the same time the Saint Louis, Des Moines and Northern was being built, Hubbell's Narrow Gauge Railway Construction Co. was working on another project, from Des Moines to Fonda. That was leased to the Wabash, Saint Louis and Pacific, a company which involved some big-time railroaders, including Iowan Grenville Dodge. Hubbell helped to found new towns that sprang up along the just completed railroad. In 1881 he helped plat Runnells, east of Des Moines.

It was about this time that what was perhaps Hubbell's stroke of railroading genius unfolded—the formation of the Des Moines Union Railway Co. The ''railroad'' was entirely in Des Moines and had only several miles of track. But the operation became so valuable that it was the subject of a multimillion dollar legal battle lasting for decades and going all the way to the U.S. Supreme Court. The history of the Des Moines Union Railway, which still plays a role in the Hubbell fortune, will be discussed later in this book. Not all of Hubbell's railroading interests were in Iowa, though. In uncharacteristic fashion, he invested in faraway properties as the railroad mystique tempted him. F.M.'s eldest son Frederick Cooper played a major role in those investments. As one historian put it: ''By the 1880s, with eldest son Frederick C. at his side, Hubbell was promoting and developing railroads in the Southwest, chiefly Texas. He was a major factor in building the Kansas City, Mexico and Orient out of Kansas City through Kansas, Oklahoma, and Texas to the Mexican border; the Gulf and Interstate; and the Texas Southern. At one time he owned 55 percent of the outstanding bonds of the latter line, which eventually was to become part of the Rock Island system. The other two railroads in time became units of the Santa Fe system. So closely was Hubbell involved in Texas railroading that his son lived for a number of years in Houston and Beaumont, and Hubbell himself spent many months in that state.'' But Hubbell never lost sight of opportunities in Des Moines. He knew he would be staying in the capital city with his lucrative investments in Equitable Life Insurance Co. and in land. That is why Hubbell jumped at the chance to buy Terrace Hill as the permanent roost from which to rule an empire. It was a roost befitting a man who was to go down in history as Iowa's wealthiest.

Above: Majestic even in its snow-shrouded state, the 85-foot-plus tower is probably Terrace Hill's most striking feature.

Left: A decorative canopy extending over the reception room's north windows.

Top left: After years of waiting . . . the music room has been nearly restored to its original splendor as can be seen at the end of the east-west hallway. Above: The family room or sitting room is the cheeriest room on the first floor because it is located in the southeast corner and has six windows. Originally these windows were even more heavily draped in addition to having built-in, foldaway shutters. The furniture is mostly from Governor William Larrabee's estate, with the exception of the Lincoln sewing stand. Bottom left: Ever changing, the dining room as seen in July, 1978 still boasts a richly carved oak wainscoting and built-in breakfront. Left: Crowning the grand stair is this nine by eleven-foot stained glass window, virtually flawless.

Watercolor by former Iowan, David Coolidge, Warrentown, Pennsylvania.

David Coolidge

Top: The carriage house would be considered by some even more interesting architecturally than Terrace Hill. Originally it housed horses and carriages. An icehouse was within the northernmost part of the building (not shown completely). Above: On a clear day—you can see for miles in almost any direction from either of these turrets which ascend above the rooftop.

Top left: In the reception room is one of the two salmon-colored marble fireplace mantels. (The marble is similar to Red Verona marble quarried in Verona, Italy.) Detailed brass cornices complement the modern lambrequin window treatments. Center left: The reception room as seen in the summer of 1978. Bottom left: From the drawing room one can look into the mantel mirror of the reception room across the hall and see a reflection of what seems to be an eternity of chandeliers. A pier mirror in the drawing room (not shown) contributes to this effect. Above: *Rebecca at the Well* adds a graceful dimension to any mantelshelf.

Chapter Nine

The Hubbell Mansion

Not just anybody would have bought Terrace Hill from B.F. Allen. That includes a lot of people who possessed the $60,000 that Hubbell paid for the mansion. As Hubbell's biographer noted: ''Only such a man as Fred Hubbell would have bought Terrace Hill in the first place. Only a man of his temperament and background would have cherished the home so much as to insist on its preservation over the span of a century or more. Only a strong estate would have been capable of bearing that burden of maintaining such a home all those years. . . . Fred Hubbell loved Terrace Hill as he loved his family. He took care to provide for the old place as if it were another heir.'' When Hubbell and his wife Frances signed the deed to the mansion on May 9, 1884, they paid Allen $20,000 down. The remainder of the purchase price was to be paid in this way—$5,000 within one year and the remaining $35,000 within ten years. By May 11, Hubbell and his brother-in-law H. DeVere Thompson were out visiting the mansion. On August 20, the Hubbell family began moving into the mansion. On August 23, F.M. and his son Frederick slept there for a night. The next evening, Frances Hubbell slept there, too.

By 1885, the Hubbells had established a substantial household at Terrace Hill. Census records showed the residents as F.M. (who listed his occupation as ''real estate agent''), wife Frances, children Frederick, Beulah, and Grover, plus Alice Donoghue, Katie Harkin, and Amelia Heill, all domestics; and John O'Neill, Peter Lyons, and Patrick Ryan, all laborers. The first tax bill was $600 annually. During 1885, Hubbell and Allen renegotiated the mortgage. By then, Hubbell had already paid $10,000 of the $40,000, twice as much as he was obligated to. Allen signed the revised mortgage as president of the Monarch Insurance Co. of Des Moines. Monarch, established the year before, was involved in the original mortgage. (Iowa Insurance Department records showed that Monarch went out of business after three years of existence. The reason for the downfall and Allen's role in it were not stated.) By 1891, the Hubbells had paid off the renegotiated mortgage, which meant they owned the mansion free and clear.

Hubbell did not leave the house as it had been under Allen's ownership. Simpson Smith, who after F.M.'s death was an administrator of the estate, said one of the first changes was the addition of a stained glass window at the head of the grand staircase. That has been disputed, however, by the mansion's current-day architect, who believes the window was original. The shape of the window lends itself to the hallway; it looks too appropriate to be an afterthought. There has been no dispute, though, about other matters. An elaborate crystal chandelier and bronze light fixtures were installed at Terrace Hill shortly after the Hubbells took occupancy. A heating plant was built in the carriage house. Prior to that, the only heat in Terrace Hill came from eight fireplaces and some wood-burning stoves. Hubbell also replaced the roof reservoir that was dependent on rain water with an up-to-date plumbing system. Some of the changes were reflected in an undated estimate of the mansion's value that was probably prepared not long after Hubbell purchased Terrace Hill. It may have been prepared by Hubbell himself. The five-page document showed a total value of slightly over $55,000. Because that was so close to the actual purchase price, it was possible that the document was an attempt to justify what Hubbell had paid for the mansion. Whatever its purpose, the document was of interest, and occasionally revealing. It was divided into these categories: brickwork, stonework, cement work, lumber, cornices, tin work, plastering, windows, doors, stairs, porches, floors, elevators, mantels and grates, wainscoting, plumbing, basement vault, steam heating, and others. The document indicated that the house had sixty window screens, fifty-five storm windows, two porches, two canopies, a passenger elevator, and a dumb-waiter.

The Hubbells did not think of Terrace Hill as a museum, or as an inviolate family sanctuary. Rather, it was used for all manner of social functions. Every year Hubbell gave a dinner party to entertain members of the Des Moines City Council. He did it even though there was no love lost between him and most Council members. In fact, when Hubbell tried to get his way in municipal affairs, he had difficulty. Part of the reason was the discord over ownership of the water system. But that was temporarily forgotten at the dinners, which were sometimes followed by poker games. After Hubbell started playing poker regularly rather late in life, he became attached to it. The games were for money, but stakes were not high—Hubbell attained his wealth in ways big and small by taking gambles, but never major gambles. In 1895, Hubbell threw a party at Terrace Hill to celebrate the fortieth anniversary of his arrival in Fort Des Moines. He shared the occasion with other pioneers, including P.M. Casady, Hoyt Sherman, J.S. Polk, James Savery, and Edwin Clapp. His diary for that day said ''Dinner at 7. Dispersed at 10 P.M. Good time, they said. Wanted me to send for them at the end of another forty years.''

The 1895 Census showed F.M. and Frances living in the mansion with two of their three children. Frederick C. had moved out, although he had brought his wife to live at Terrace Hill for awhile after their wedding. Their first child—F.M.'s first grandchild—was born in 1891 at Terrace Hill. The child was named Frederick Windsor Hubbell. The 1895 Census listed four other people living in the house. All four appeared to be relatives on Mrs. Hubbell's side. No domestic help was listed, but there was surely some, whether residing in the mansion or not. In the 1905 Census, there were at least a dozen employees living in the mansion.

Two gala events took place at Terrace Hill as the nineteenth century drew to a close. The first was in 1897, when the Hubbells opened Terrace Hill to 500 guests gathered in Des Moines for a women's suffrage convention. Some of the leading suffragettes in America were in attendance. One newspaper account described the gathering: ''Five hundred people responded to the invitations of Mr. and Mrs. F.M. Hubbell to meet the noted women attending the suffrage convention last evening. The guests were received by Mr. and Mrs. Hubbell, Mrs. Hubbell beautifully gowned in black and white striped satin brocaded in roses, with vest and stock of pale blue satin. . . . The evening was entirely informal. The Des Moines ladies entertained charmingly. Mrs. Dr. Potter (sic) and Miss Marie Stewart invited the guests to the dining room, where coffee and confections were served from a table beautifully decorated in yellow and blue. The centerpiece consisted of an immense jardiniere of yellow jonquils resting on yellow embroidered linen and set off by burning white tapers in tall candelabra. Miss Beulah Hubbell, in pearl silk trimmed in sable, presided over the punch bowl.'' F.M. seemed to be an advocate of women's rights. In a 1914 statement, Hubbell said: ''I hope to live long enough to see women given every right men have. Men know that women are better. They are educated. They own property. Why should they not have equal rights? I want to see women vote because they will vote to improve many things that ought to be improved. I do not want to pose as a prohibitionist, but the saloon will be abolished someday, and the women's vote will do it.''

The second gala event, just before the turn of the century, rivaled the Allens' 1869 housewarming for opulence. The occasion was the marriage of F.M. and Frances' daughter Beulah Hubbell to Swedish count Carl Wachtmeister. The couple had met in Chicago, where he was secretary of the Swedish consulate. Terrace Hill was probably one of the few private residences in the country large enough to accommodate all the guests, and grand enough to be truly appropriate. An enthusiastic account of the ceremony was written by a reporter from the *Des Moines Leader,* who posed as a foreign diplomat to gain admittance. He was not discovered among the 700 invited guests. The reporter termed the wedding ''the most notable social event in Des Moines' history, uniting the scion of an ancient and noble continental line to the daughter of a wealthy American family.'' The guests included nobles from several European nations, members of the Des Moines aristocracy, and ''noteworthy'' people from Chicago, Washington D.C., and other cities where Beulah Hubbell had mixed in the upper reaches of society. The ceremony itself was termed ''the crowning glory of the life of the fair bride.'' The description

Frances Hubbell and daughter Beulah. (Courtesy Mary Belle Hubbell Windsor.)

was filled with hyperbole, but painted what was probably the picture perceived by many in attendance: "Under the shimmering, many-tinted lights of the great parlor chandelier, with its thousands of cut-glass prisms before an altar of ferns and lilies, with the melodious strains of the Lohengrin wedding march floating softly through the hallways on the perfume-laden air, the happy couple spoke the vows which united ancient title and beauty, wealth and ancestral honor, the offspring of ancient nobility and the scion of modern progressiveness and enterprise." The account, calling Terrace Hill a "palace," said the great hall of the house "seemed almost lonesome while the bridal party was forming for its movement to the parlor in which the wedding was to take place." The bridal party formed on the landing of the imposing staircase, which was decorated with smilax entwined with bunches of white carnations. White ribbons and streamers were on the newel-posts,

Dining room shows built-in breakfront, right of butler's pantry.

The dining room as seen in the early 1900s.

and roses were in the hall below. The groom was described as "pale but composed." The bride was described as a "picture of composure, and looking happy as a bride should." Beulah Hubbell wore a white satin brocade court gown, the same one she had worn when she was presented to English royalty at the Court of St. James. The skirt and bodice were trimmed in silver, with the yoke and sleeves of white illusion. The court train was made of brocaded satin, and had ruffles of chiffon falling from the shoulders. There were many gifts to open after the ceremony, of course. F.M.'s gift to his daughter—a dowry of sorts—was a $200,000 ten-year note paying 4 percent interest, or $8,000 annually.

Photographs taken the day of the wedding showed how parts of the mansion looked. In the dining room was a door opening into a large butler's pantry equipped with a sink, icebox, warming stove, serving counter, and dumbwaiter used to carry prepared food from the ground floor kitchen to the first floor dining room, which contained a massive built-in buffet and ornate shelving over the marble fireplace. If it can be said that Allen spared no expense in building the mansion, it can also fairly be said that Hubbell was willing to spend large sums to improve it. In 1900, Hubbell, with his characteristic thoroughness, decided—for reasons unknown—to prepare an inventory of every item in the house. He eventually included 592 items. Following is a sampling from that list:

- Music room—a mahogany chair with velour upholstery, two small Persian rugs, an Angora goat rug, and an onyx ostrich egg.
- Dining room—a Champlain marble fireplace with oak mantel glass, a brass fire set, and a red and gold Venetian glass punch bowl.
- West Room—a Romeo and Juliet statue on a marble pedestal, an oil painting titled *The Last Days of the Venetian Republic* and a glass ornament.
- Lower Hall—two carved oak chairs, a carved rosewood table, a Chinese embroidered centerpiece, a Dresden vase, a Turkish silk gold-embroidered banner, an inlaid table, a Japanese bronze jardiniere, a steel engraving of Washington Irving, a large Chinese bronze vase, and portraits of Mrs. Hubbell's parents.
- Library—a mahogany secretary, a Chinese lacquer plaque, a cherry rocker, a tall bronze with dragons, a Japanese bell, a Chinese cloisonne vase, an enameled tea strainer, and a picture of the house's master, F.M. Hubbell.
- Parlor—a Satsuma vase, a miniature of Beulah Hubbell, an ornamental thermometer, a Venetian glass lamp, a German drinking mug, and a large French bowl with red flowers and bird decorations.

In the inventory many units were included as one item—for example, forty-eight blue-and-gold dinner plates with platters to match. While the Hubbells have rarely been accused of flaunting their wealth, no one has ever claimed that they lived the simple life of monks either.

Drawing room with massive chandelier reflecting in pier mirror.

Corner closets on either side of main hall looking northward.

Dissecting hall which leads west to music room.

Music room as seen from the drawing room.

Photographs of the Terrace Hill interior were all taken in the
very late nineteenth century. (Courtesy William Wagner.)

Chapter Ten

Expanding an Empire

To generate the money that allowed the family to maintain its fabulous life-style, Hubbell never stopped looking for lucrative opportunities. He found plenty of them. In the last two decades of the 1800s and on past 1900, Hubbell concentrated on new railroad ventures, getting out when prospects appeared dim, or, alternately, selling when there was a profit to be made. Hubbell also consolidated his land and insurance holdings. And, perhaps most significant, he took an ingenious step to preserve his wealth through the generations.

First, the railroading ventures. Hubbell's railroad dealings were so complex that they were often hard to unravel. But they are such a key to his fortune that at least a simplified version is vital to an understanding of the man and his massive estate. On December 29, 1898, an entry in Hubbell's diary said that he had sold a number of railroad bonds to the Chicago, Milwaukee and St. Paul Railroad Co. for a total of $1,827,500. The sale was the culmination of Hubbell's success with narrow gauge railroads in Iowa. What Hubbell sold on that date was the Des Moines, Northern and Western Railroad Co., of which he and his son Frederick C. were the top officers. The company had forty-two miles of road from Des Moines to Boone and another 107 miles from Clive to Fonda. The company resulted in 1892 from the consolidation of several lines. In its first year of operation, it took in $406,000. In the year before it was sold, the gross was $503,000. Those sums were small compared with the income of the national roads. Yet Hubbell knew he owned property the giants wanted, so he hung on to it until the time to sell was right.

When the Des Moines, Northern and Western was sold, it ended an era in Hubbell's life, the era of frenetic dealings in narrow gauge railroading. Why did he sell? Hubbell's biographer speculated: "For two reasons, probably. One was that he may have decided the future was not bright for the smaller independent railroad. The nation's big railroad systems were well established by that time. The advantages of large-scale rail operations were apparent. Secondly, Hubbell never liked having his interests spread all over the country. When he sold the Fonda and Boone lines, he almost completely returned to Des Moines, so far as his business interests were concerned."

Hubbell had not left railroading altogether. He remained involved with three Des Moines terminal companies that served giant carriers for the rest of his life. The companies were the Des Moines Union Railway, organized in the mid-1880s; the Des Moines Western Railway, formed in 1902; and the Des Moines Terminal Co., also begun in the first years of the twentieth century. All told, the three railroads operated fewer than ten miles of track. So, one might reasonably ask, why did major lines fight the Hubbells for decades, all the way to the U.S. Supreme Court, over the question of who was to control that mileage?

Before attempting to understand the controversy, it is helpful to understand more about the terminal companies, especially the key one—the Des Moines Union. A history in the 1896 Iowa Board of Railroad Commissioners report said the Des Moines Union was conceived in 1882 by executives of the Des Moines and Saint Louis Railroad Co., the Des Moines Northwestern Railway Co., and the Saint Louis, Des Moines and Northern Railway Co. A contract was signed to create a union depot and trackage to be operated in and around Des Moines. But the flesh was not put on the bones of the contract until 1884, when F.M. Hubbell, J.S. Polk, Grenville Dodge, and several other members of the Iowa aristocracy met. Dodge was named president; Hubbell became secretary-treasurer. The company was to operate "from the easterly limits of the city of Des Moines to its westerly limits, being a distance of four miles." The Des Moines Union later built an extension from the main track near West Twelfth Street south to the Raccoon River, then east across Ninth Street and north and south parallel to Ninth Street. There were also extensions from the main track on the east side of the river to the starch works, the stockyards, the packing house, and the malt house. In 1896, when the railroad commissioners published their history, Frederick C. Hubbell was president of the Des Moines Union. F.M. was secretary. A.B. Cummins and H.D. Thompson, both of whom had close ties to the Hubbells, were the other officers.

The challenge to the Hubbells' control of the terminal line began in 1907. When it reached the U.S. Supreme Court in 1920, the Hubbells were still in control, even though the family patriarch had passed the age of eighty. The challengers in the legal battle were the Wabash Railroad Co. and the Chicago, Milwaukee and Saint Paul Railway Co. The Wabash was the successor to the Des Moines and Saint Louis line, one of the three roads that had been a party to the incorporation of the Des Moines Union back in 1884. The Chicago, Milwaukee and St. Paul was the successor to the other two lines present at the creation. When the lawsuit was filed, the two complaining railroads owned three-eighths of the stock in the Des Moines Union. The Hubbells laid claim to five-eighths. The main issue was simple: Did the Hubbells own majority control themselves, thus being entitled to the profits? That was the stance the Hubbells took. Or, were the Hubbells simply trustees, there to run the Des Moines Union for the benefit of the two major railroads that used its facilities?

The trial court decision was unsatisfactory to both sides, so both appealed. The appeals court ruled for the Hubbells. But the U.S. Supreme Court reversed the decision, hinting that the wily Hubbells had taken unfair advantage of less intelligent businessmen while gaining control of the company. The Hubbells were ordered to surrender their stock.

The litigation was not entirely resolved until 1932, because there were separate court actions concerning the Hubbells' Des Moines Terminal Co., which performed the same functions as the Des Moines Union, but which operated separately. The Des Moines Terminal Co. tracks joined the Des Moines Union tracks, yet had been built independently to serve the Factory Addition where Hubbell owned so much industrial property. Two major railroads—the Chicago, Burlington and Quincy, and the Chicago Great Western—had joined with the two railroads fighting the Hubbells in the Des Moines Union case to claim ownership of Factory Addition trackage.

In 1931, a federal appeals court said the railroads controlling the Des Moines Union had a right to use the tracks that had been built by the Des Moines Terminal Co. But, because the terminal company tracks were clearly owned by the Hubbells, the court ruled that the major railroads would have to pay the Hubbells for use of the track. In 1932, the U.S. Supreme Court refused to review the case. By the time everything was settled, F.M. Hubbell was dead, but he probably would have been satisfied with the outcome: The tracks and equipment owned by the Hubbells were placed under a perpetual lease to the railroads that had won control of the Des Moines Union.

The third Des Moines terminal operation established by the Hubbells was not nearly so controversial. It was the Des Moines Western Railway Co., which operated several miles of track in east Des Moines. It was originally established to serve the Des Moines, Iowa Falls and Northern Railway as it ran between the capital city and Iowa Falls. The Des Moines Western stayed in the Hubbell family until 1973, when it was sold to the Fort Dodge, Des Moines and Southern Railway Co.

Hubbell's insurance dealings, unlike his railroad activities, were never successfully challenged. And in the end it was Hubbell's ownership of Equitable Life that was the cornerstone of his wealth. Hubbell did not assume the presidency of the company he had founded in 1867 until 1888. By then Equitable Life was on solid footing, thanks to Hoyt Sherman, who had served as president since Allen had been compelled to step down in 1874. By 1888 Equitable Life had relocated in an office near the Polk County Courthouse. It was doing business in numerous states and had a sizable sales force. Insurance policies issued totaled $2.5 million and assets topped $650,000. Hubbell, by wheeling and dealing, had acquired all but 340 of the 4,000 shares of stock, giving him undisputed control. Hubbell, however, did not become a dictator. He had too many other things on his mind to handle every problem that arose with policyholders. So he made it clear that Cyrus Kirk, an Equitable Life veteran, would be the operations chief. Hubbell

drew the top salary—$3,000 annually to Kirk's $2,400—but Hubbell did not make all the decisions. As F.M. expressed his philosophy to Kirk in a conversation recreated in the official story of Equitable Life: "Twenty-one years ago, when I was a mere boy, I started this company with not much more to back me than the optimism of youth, a fair knowledge of the theory of life insurance, and the blessing of Judge Casady. I had lots of irons heating in those days, so when I got some stock sold, and the state issued us a charter, I persuaded Major Sherman to manage this business while I minded other things. I was pretty young, but I had learned that a successful enterprise is mainly a marriage of men and money, especially good men. So from the first I have tried to get men to work for me who are smarter than I am. I then make it my business to support them with the money and other things they need to get on with the job . . . . I suppose I pretty much own this company, but I have no desire to run it."

During Hubbell's nineteen-year term as president, the company grew significantly. Equitable Life's assets increased from about $650,000 to $12.4 million while Hubbell was president. Insurance in force increased from $2.5 million to $34.8 million. The gains occurred despite outside adverse influences that had to be overcome. For example, the nationwide financial panic of 1893 hurt Equitable Life's business—when people are unemployed, they are less likely to buy insurance. Furthermore, the company, conservative in its practices, was sometimes at a disadvantage when competing against more reckless insurers that promised the world at a low price. But Equitable Life picked up customers, as it became clear that the flashier insurers could not always deliver on their promises. So, when Hubbell decided to retire as president in 1907 at age sixty-eight, the company was in good shape. Hubbell's personal fortune was in good shape, too, as he and family members continued to hold all but a small portion of the Equitable Life stock. In 1923, the family finally succeeded in obtaining the small portion of the stock that had eluded them, purchasing the holdings of the heirs of Absalom Morris. A Fort Des Moines pioneer, Morris had been Equitable Life's first general insurance agent.

While the Hubbells were gaining total control of the company, Equitable Life was putting on a more imposing front to the public. In 1891, it moved from a small office on Courthouse Square to a larger building. Then, in 1907, the company left its rented quarters to move into its own office. The Hubbells had spent $286,000 for an eight-story structure at the northwest corner of Sixth and Locust streets.

It was in 1919 that the company made a move to develop the most impressive facade of all. Equitable Life bought the quarter-block on the southwest corner of Sixth and Locust streets. The land, which had a number of existing buildings on it, cost $485,000 plus another $153,000 required to purchase leases. Actually, no money changed hands, because the land had been owned by Bankers Trust Co. To get it, Equitable

Life traded its home office building to the bank. It was probably the biggest real estate deal in Des Moines' history up until then.

Equitable Life decided to raze the buildings on its newly acquired site and construct an eighteen-story gothic edifice with a seven-story tower. It was finished in 1924. The company's official story noted: "If ever a building mirrored the image of a corporation, the new home of the company was and is a steel and stone reflection of Equitable of Iowa—sound, solid and conservative." By that time, F.M. was not as spry as he used to be. But he remained involved in Equitable Life's affairs until his last year; he was never a man to be ignored. Five months before his death at the age of ninety-one, Hubbell summoned Henry Nollen, Equitable Life's president, to Terrace Hill. The stock market crash of 1929 had occurred. The insurer was in trouble. At Terrace Hill, propped up erect on his bed, Hubbell gave Nollen this advice, as recreated in the company history: "Henry, you are heading into heavy seas. The market collapse last fall started a depression which may last a very long time. You must be prepared for times more troubled than any you have ever seen. Forty years ago when Hoyt retired and I turned the company over to Kirk, I asked only one thing of him

Jefferson S. Polk. (Courtesy Iowa State Historical Department.)

—that he always make sure he managed things so as to be able and ready to pay all claims whenever due. He did. Then years ago when war and flu assailed us I asked you to make sure we could weather the storm and you did, even though some of your associates thought your methods harsh. Now, I think, you face the sternest test of all. Remember, Henry, I'm depending on you to run things so whatever happens, Equitable will still be right here in Des Moines one hundred years from today, able and ready to pay all claims."

None of this is meant to give the impression that Hubbell's business life was concerned exclusively with railroading and Equitable Life. Hubbell was in the midst of many other dealings. Some of the stormiest involved Jefferson Polk. Although the lucrative partnership had survived many travails, there were always rumors of a split. Some of the rumors had a kernel of truth behind them. For instance, in early 1883 Hubbell wrote in his diary: "Polk came to the office tonight to talk over the future of our firm. He wanted to know if I wanted to dissolve. I told him no."

The partnership did break up, in 1887. In the meantime, the two men had purchased B.F. Allen's assets from bankruptcy court and made other profitable moves so characteristic of them. As Iowa pioneer lawyer and state legislator Edward Stiles characterized the partners: "Polk possessed great acumen and a natural legal mind . . . I heard him frequently spoken of as one of the most promising young lawyers in the state. . . . He entered into partnership with F.M. Hubbell under the firm name Polk and Hubbell. Mr. Hubbell might in some respects be likened unto the late Mr. Harriman, the railroad promoter and money-maker. Mr. Hubbell was naturally a money getter on safe lines, rather than a lawyer. Thus constituted, the firm of Polk and Hubbell was for years a leading factor in the financial life and public interests of Des Moines."

When Polk and Hubbell did part ways, it was not friendly. It took them two years to settle on how to divide their property. On January 10, 1888, Hubbell headed one of his diary pages "Memo of Polk's unjust and unfair treatment to me." Listed were seven grievances, including the division of Equitable Life stock, the amount of payments by Hubbell to Polk for being a partner, and some profitable dealings by Polk on land surrounding Terrace Hill. There were arguments over how to divide railroad and water company holdings. Polk apparently threatened Hubbell with a lawsuit if one of Hubbell's water companies tried to do business in a certain area. Hubbell's diary said: "I told Polk we intended only to supply the suburbs of Des Moines with water and if he interfered with that, we should lock horns. He reminded me of the fable of the wolf and the lamb and wanted me to consider him the lamb." When a settlement was reached, Hubbell seemed satisfied. One diary page said, "I get Polk's water stock $105,000, his railroad stock subject to (Grenville) Dodge's interest $500,000, the Westfall judgment $9,000, lots at Herndon, right of way, etc."

Those who have studied Hubbell's character have not found it surprising that he fell out with Polk, despite their lucrative partnership. "Few indeed were they with whom F.M. did not disagree, sometimes violently, at one time or another," wrote one historian. "After all, a man who at twenty-two could write 'I would not trust another's judgment as soon as my own' is bound to differ with his fellows. Only the Judge (Casady), whom F.M. looked to as a father, and (Hoyt) Sherman, whom he relied on as a brother, knew nothing but harmony in their relationship with him."

When Hubbell and Polk separated, F.M. did not waste time figuring out how to reorganize his business interests. He established F.M. Hubbell, Son and Co., Inc., which still exists today. The original partners were Hubbell himself, his son Frederick C., and H. DeVere Thompson, his business associate and in-law.

The water company, which Hubbell helped form in 1871, demanded his attention. Hubbell traveled the country, selling Des Moines water bonds. His diary said that on one day, he sold $10,000 in bonds to one Cleveland, Ohio, man and ordered an additional $32,000 worth sent by express. The same week, Hubbell sold $15,000 worth to a Cleveland savings bank. Hubbell owned a substantial amount of water company securities himself. Because the city and private buyers were expressing interest in obtaining the water company, Hubbell gave thought to what terms he might exact. In 1888, he wrote, "I want water free always. I want the right to put in stock at a price up to $500,000. I want one-third of the profits on any new reorganization of works. I want the purchaser to guarantee sale of new bonds at a price not lower than ninety-five. I want my side to have one-third of all salaries and perquisites and the right to buy new stock or bonds at the same price as sold to others and to take one-third thereof at my option. I want a contract to protect me so they will have to make me an offer to give or take whenever I want them to. I want a contract to light my house. I want ten thousand dollars of second mortgage bonds and all of my floating debts taken care of." Hubbell was involved in other water companies, too. They served separate communities such as North Des Moines, Greenwood Park, and University Place that are now part of the city of Des Moines.

By the mid-1890s, Hubbell had sold some of his stock in the Des Moines Water Co., but the Hubbell family never stopped being involved in company ownership until the city takeover in 1919. Management passed in part, however, to out-of-state interests. On July 20, 1897, Hubbell was replaced as president of the company by John Cole of Chicago. Many of the new directors were from Portland, Maine, where a syndicate of buyers was based. But even during the 1919 election where Des Moines voters finally approved the city take over, the elderly Hubbell could not keep out of the news—understandably, since he stood to make money on his water company holdings if the sale price were high enough. The amount finally approved was $3,450,000. Hubbell's diary one day in 1919 noted that he was scolded by son Frederick C. "because I told a reporter that I was going to vote for the purchase of the waterworks and that they were worth a million dollars more than the city was paying for them."

Hubbell's real estate was becoming increasingly lucrative by the end of the 1890s, as the growth of Des Moines led to a heightened demand for commercial land. Hubbell owned what were considered to be prime commercial building sites. An 1899 list of building improvements in the city showed $50,000 spent by Hubbell interests on the Victoria Hotel at Sixth and Chestnut streets, and another $18,000 spent on the Seventh and Vine business block. A few years later, records showed that Hubbell bought a building at Eighth and Walnut streets for $190,000, and put up a new building nearby soon thereafter. A contemporary of Hubbell's who was also growth-oriented commented that F.M. "stands ready to erect other buildings for industries seeking a place in a city which does things." Hubbell said much the same thing in his own words in a 1908 magazine article, writing: "To promote manufacturing interests in Des Moines, we must be hospitable to the outside manufacturer who seeks a location. Give him the glad hand. Help him to get land or rent it to him reasonably. Take stock if necessary to assist him in that way. Then buy his goods and stand by him in every way."

To increase his fortune so as to live in Terrace Hill in the most comfortable manner possible, Hubbell even tried his hand at controlling some Des Moines banks. Newspaper advertisements in 1902 showed F.M. as a director of the Des Moines National Bank and the Valley National Bank. He owned stock in several—for instance, 20 percent of the Capital City State Bank in 1910, and almost half by 1912. But Hubbell failed in at least three attempts to gain a seat on that bank's board of directors.

By the turn of the century, Hubbell's wealth was legendary. Perhaps most people did not understand the vastness of Hubbell's empire, however, until 1903, when he established a trust for his property. The purpose was to preserve his wealth not only for the remainder of his lifetime (he was sixty-four), but for his heirs as well. Terrace Hill—the most visible reminder of Hubbell's fortune, the possession dearest to him—was singled out for special attention in what proved to be an ingenious trust document.

Chapter Eleven

The Hubbell Trust

On March 18, 1903, at a meeting of the Equitable Life Insurance board of trustees, Hubbell told the eight other persons assembled at Terrace Hill he had decided to put everything he owned into a trust. It would guard his possessions as long as the law allowed—twenty-one years after the death of his last direct heir. The terms were prepared under Hubbell's direction by attorney J.C. Hume. The thirty-two page document not only contained warnings to Hubbell's descendants about becoming spendthrifts, but also made it difficult for them to do so. The document had three sections: Schedule A, which listed property not to be sold; Schedule B, which listed property that could be sold; and Schedule C, which dealt with Hubbell's personal effects. Terrace Hill, not surprisingly, was singled

F. M. Hubbell. (Courtesy Iowa State Historical Department.)

out to be kept within the family. The trust document said the mansion "shall be and remain the homestead of the Hubbell family, and in the possession of the eldest male lineal descendant (of F.M. and Frances) so long as any such descendant lives, during the whole of the trust period." In 1903, not many tycoons had taken the care to insure for the future that Hubbell took. His trust was so restrictive and long-lasting as to be highly unusual. Some experts said the document was unique. As a result, a court test was sought: The Hubbell family would breathe easier if it knew that what F.M. had done to preserve his wealth were legal. In 1907, the Iowa Supreme Court agreed to decide the legality of the trust. The test case turned on a specific question: Did the document give the trustees the power to sign a lease for a period that might exceed the life of the trust? But the justices went beyond the specific question to comment on F.M. Hubbell's document in its entirety. The ruling noted that the courts had no particular interest in seeing wealthy men design ways to retain that wealth beyond the grave. The court added, however, that neither should it interfere in the retention of wealth within a family if the acts of the trusts were not in conflict with state or federal law.

"Proverbially the accumulations of the provident never reach the fourth generation," the ruling said, noting that Hubbell hoped to demonstrate the proverb wrong. "If in recognition of this, or because of the distrust of the business sagacity of those on whom he would bestow his bounty, the owner elects to tie up his estate during the period of lives then in being and twenty-one years thereafter by conveying it to trustees," he has the right to do so. After the Supreme Court ruling upholding the trust, it attracted attention far beyond Iowa. When Hubbell died in 1930, his obituary in the *New York Times* devoted more space to the trust than to any other of the multimillionaire's accomplishments. The obituary said, "In 1903, Mr. Hubbell created the first long-time trust devised in Iowa and took every precaution to protect it from legal attack by relatives not beneficiaries. It was unique and so perfectly drawn that it attracted worldwide attention. Into the original fund he is said to have put $2 million, leaving it open so that he might add to it. This he did in later years, until the fund was several times the original amount. He limited the fund to all the beneficiaries then living, which included himself and his wife, their children and grandchildren. It was provided that the fund should run for twenty-one years and nine months after the death of the last beneficiary, which, according to the tables of probability of life, would terminate the fund about the year 2000. To keep the document from being broken by other relatives, it included a provision that in the event of the deaths of all the beneficiaries, the estate should go to the state of Iowa."

The trust that attracted worldwide attention did not last until the year 2000. The expiration date turned out to be 1983. Terrace Hill was separated from the trust before then, of course, but that it stayed in the Hubbell family for as long as it did was a tribute to the careful drafting of the document. One thing was certain—while F.M. Hubbell was still alive, he enjoyed his mansion to the fullest. In his later years, the house was the site of tributes to its master. In 1905, there was a party for Hubbell to celebrate the fiftieth anniversary of his arrival in Des Moines. One newspaper noted that Hubbell's "holdings of Des Moines property are larger than those of any other man in the city, and he is known to be the city's largest taxpayer. He has been active in building up some of the most successful institutions of Des Moines and in securing factories and new industries." In 1912, on Hubbell's seventy-third birthday, there was an even bigger party at Terrace Hill. Attorney Jim Weaver read aloud a twenty-stanza laudatory poem. It traced Hubbell's life from his boyhood in Connecticut to his venerable, powerful old age.

Hubbell was clearly a powerful man. Rarely was a negative word printed or spoken about him in places that he might see it or hear of it. The newspapers ran articles on his birthday, and even editorials of congratulation. A 1912 news article ran under the headline

HUBBELL AT 73RD MILEPOST OF LIFE

Birthday Anniversary Finds
Famous Iowa Capitalist
in Fine Fettle.

HEALTH IS BEST GIFT

Glad to Be Alive and in
Position to Do
Good.

The article estimated Hubbell's wealth at tens of millions of dollars. In 1922, on Hubbell's eighty-third birthday, there was a stag party at Terrace Hill. Hubbell said that if he had retired at age seventy, as some prominent men were doing, he might not have lived to be eighty-three. "Idleness kills" was the gist of his wisdom.

Decades before his death, Hubbell was being praised profusely by business leaders, historians, and journalists alike. One collection of biographical sketches covering prominent Des Moines people said of Hubbell: "The success that he has achieved is almost beyond belief. He has come into possession of a large portion of the most valuable property of the city.

Upon this he has erected many fine buildings and has plans in view which will still further beautify the city. There is probably not another man in Des Moines that has done so much for its development and prosperity, as he is ever ready to lend his support to any enterprise which he believes calculated to prove of public benefit. He usually supports the Democratic Party but is not a politician, and in local affairs votes for the man whom he deems best qualified for office regardless of party lines. He is a man of firm conviction and is a worthy representative of that type of American citizenship which has done so much toward the development of the Middle West."

Hubbell was not always in Des Moines cutting business deals or celebrating anniversaries at Terrace Hill. He traveled a lot—sometimes even for pleasure. Probably the longest trip he took was in 1892, with Oliver Perkins, the bachelor half-brother of Hubbell's brother-in-law H.D. Thompson. Hubbell's diary indicated that the two men visited Australia, Hawaii, Samoa, and England. Even on the pleasure trip, though, he could not refrain from conducting some business. When in London Hubbell called on bankers to learn if they were interested in selling American railroad bonds. Most of Hubbell's trips away from Des Moines did not cover so much territory, and were usually for specific purposes. In 1894, Hubbell went to Washington D.C. to use his influence in successfully obtaining the Des Moines postmaster's appointment for E.H. Hunter. Hubbell visited the postmaster general and talked with an aide to President Grover Cleveland at the White House. This was not his only brush with politics, either. Hubbell never tried to attain important political offices himself, but he believed in helping those who were his friends, or whose politics were compatible with his own. In 1901, Hubbell publicly supported his friend and legal counselor Albert Cummins for Iowa governor. In 1912, Hubbell escorted presidential candidate Woodrow Wilson around Des Moines. Hubbell also lent his energies to causes that were charitable or community-oriented. In the 1890s he became president of the Des Moines Home for the Aged, a position he retained until near his death. He was chairman of a group organized in the 1890s to raise money to buy land for an army post in Des Moines—the land was purchased, donated to the federal government, and a post was erected. Hubbell's generosity from time to time was recognized: In 1909, a public school was named in his honor. In the 1920s, after a struggle spanning decades, Hubbell convinced the City Council of the wisdom of building a diagonal thoroughfare. Hubbell donated a strip of land for the street, spending tens of thousands of dollars of his own money to get his way. Resistance was great, partly because many people believed there must be a hidden profit for Hubbell. Hubbell's biographer, however, saw the campaign for the diagonal road as one based on common sense, not greed. "If Hubbell anticipated a major real estate boom in that area, he was disappointed," wrote George Mills. "No big expansion of real estate values came to pass. His thinking was much broader than day-by-day real estate prices in one section of the city. His major purpose in promoting the street might be stated this way: 'What's good for Des Moines is good for me.''' One motive was the saving of travel time, an important consideration to a man for whom time was money. He was pleased, he once said, that travelers coming into Des Moines from the northeast could reach their destinations faster, ''as long as they don't spend those extra hours wastefully.'' The thoroughfare was named Avenue Frederick M. Hubbell. The road eventually drew praise. One newspaper commented, ''Mr. Hubbell has done a service to the city that will be more fully appreciated as time passes, one that nobody but himself would have thought of doing, and that nobody but himself would have done.''

Hubbell traveled the city, by foot and automobile, with regularity. A *Register* columnist reported, ''Yesterday, there was F.M. Hubbell, a familiar figure on Locust Street with his light-colored bowler hat, high pointed collar and cutaway coat. He always had a paper in his hand and he was always going hell-bent as if somebody was after him.'' The columnist added that she had ''seen Mr. Hubbell being driven through town in that old Essex a hundred times.''

Whenever people dealt with Hubbell, they assumed that he was powerful. It was usually a sound assumption, if only because he often owned land that somebody else needed. Illustrative of that was an exchange of letters during 1913 between Hubbell and Grenville Dodge, who had retired to his mansion in Council Bluffs, Iowa. At the time, Dodge was a leader in the drive to expand the Capitol grounds in Des Moines. He needed Hubbell-owned property for the plan to succeed. Dodge wrote to F.M.: ''This property must be obtained for a reasonable sum, and here is where you can help us greatly. You own a good deal of property that we will have to secure, and you can set the pace on what we will have to pay for it by setting a very reasonable price on your property . . . . I know your public spirit, and the interest you have taken in the Allison Monument, and the great interest you have taken in Des Moines, and for that reason I make a personal appeal to you . . . . By taking a personal interest in it, there is no man that can have as much influence in carrying out these plans successfully as you can, and I will take it as a great personal favor if you will take hold of it and give it not only your influence, but your aid in the matter.'' Hubbell responded one week later in an understated fashion: ''I do not have very much property inside of the proposed boundaries, but for what any of us do own, we shall also do what we can to induce others to accept prices that are fair.''

During these later years in which so many people with plans came to Hubbell, he viewed the parade from Terrace Hill, with his wife Frances by his side. She was not often in the public eye, but influenced F.M. An interview on the Hubbell's fiftieth wedding anniversary in 1913 provided a forum for her views, including this passage: ''Why is dress so necessary to women? Why if a gown is good should it be cast aside because it is not the latest dictate of fashion? Where is all this going to lead? Now please do not misunderstand me. I would always want pretty things for my home, but that is what puzzles me, why is not the home and the adornment of the home woman's chief interest? It seems to me woman has branched out into so many avenues. When I was married my first thought was that we should live so that we would always have a good home, and something to keep us, and always my home has seemed to me the important issue.'' With domestic affairs in his wife's able hands, Hubbell did not have to worry much about the care of Terrace Hill. He did worry about his wife, though, because her health was not good. She suffered from asthma and other ailments. F.M. was continually searching for somebody who could ease her pain. One of his diary entries said, ''Maj. Walter S. Sharpe, M.D., and J.M. Rich of Fort Des Moines gave their treatment to Frances at 4 P.M. today. It was very beneficial, relieving her of asthma and nervous spasms. They will come again Sunday for another treatment.'' Despite Frances Hubbell's frailty, she and F.M. celebrated their sixty-first wedding anniversary with a party at Terrace Hill on March 19, 1924. She was eighty-three years old. Guests were received from 3 p.m. to 6 p.m. in the east living room, which was filled with baskets of flowers. Frances' sister Florence Cooper Ginn attended—she had also been at the wedding in 1863. There was gaiety, there were memories. But within two months, Frances was dead.

When she died, Hubbell's life changed drastically. Grover Hubbell, their youngest child, did not want the elderly patriarch to live alone. So Grover, his wife Anna and their daughters Frances, Helen Virginia, and Mary Belle moved in to Terrace Hill. Several yardmen and servants also lived in the house, assuring that F.M. would be taken care of. With Grover's occupancy in 1924, modernization of the mansion began, whether F.M. liked it or not. The cost of the remodeling reached $50,000. An elevator was installed to help the old man get from floor to floor. The heating plant was moved from the carriage house to the basement. Gas pipes were replaced with electric wires. Hubbell, who had lived in his beloved house for forty years without overhauling it, was not overjoyed at the work being spearheaded by Grover. ''A lot of men here are tearing the house to pieces according to Grover's wishes,'' Hubbell wrote in his diary. ''I don't like it. They claim to be improving it.'' After Grover's family moved in, the house was often the scene of gaiety. In the late 1920s, probably 1928, one of the city's first swimming pools was built on the grounds east of the mansion where a pond had been. It was 60 feet long, 21 feet wide and 10 feet at its greatest depth. Mary Belle Hubbell Windsor told the authors in an interview that it was so hot while the pool was being dug that horses working on the project suffered heat stroke. One died. Sometime after the pool was finished, a sculpture by Helen Virginia Hubbell was placed at the north end. The family used the pool often. Mary

Servants on southeast terrace near pond in 1890s. (Courtesy William Wagner.)

Mary Belle Hubbell Windsor, 1928. (Courtesy Mary Belle Hubbell Windsor.)

Belle recalled that when her mother Anna wanted to swim, bells rang and everyone else had to scramble out, because Anna liked the water to be absolutely calm. At the south end of the pool, behind the diving board, was a stone arched structure covered with vines that provided shade to overexposed sunbathers. Underneath it was a room from which swimmers could be observed through two windows. There was also a room housing the water pumps and an area with a lavatory and dressing facilities for the men. The women dressed in a basement room of the mansion that had a separate entrance from the outside.

One reminiscence of what life was like at Terrace Hill around that time was provided by Elmer Nelson, F.M.'s chauffeur. After Grover's family moved in, Nelson became "butler, gardener, housecleaner, etcetera, you name it," during his thirty-three years of service. The memories were conveyed to the authors in 1977 by Nelson and his daughter Frances Tometich, who were residing in North Hollywood, California. They said that they lived on the grounds in a house no longer standing. There was a telephone there with a direct connection to Terrace Hill. Mrs. Tometich said, "Never did my father complete a meal that he was not called to serve someone, either as chauffeur, errand boy, or something. Sometimes when he played butler to their parties he would get home around two or three in the morning." Nelson recalled that one evening Mary Belle Hubbell, about thirteen at the time, had a slumber party for perhaps ten friends. Nelson was summoned to Terrace Hill in the morning to clean up. He found the grand staircase covered with white down feathers from a pillow fight. Mary Belle was confined inside until she helped pick up the feathers. It seemed as if there were always parties. "The summer was our favorite, for the Hubbells had several hundred guests and they were served from tables that were gorgeous, with ice images carved with colored lights below them for centerpieces," Mrs. Tome-

Hubbell swimming pool, 1978. Note two windows for observing underwater swimmers.

tich said. "They were a sight to see. They would bring in portable dance floors, hire orchestras, and dance until the wee hours of the morning. From our little house we could look down on these garden parties that were (so) fabulous." On the Fourth of July, the Hubbells traditionally had a dinner party. When it got dark, Nelson and the housemen would shoot off fireworks. Neighbors would watch the display from the streets. At Christmas, Nelson would decorate the largest tree on the lawn in front of the house with lights. "It was a beautiful sight with snow on the ground and the huge Christmas tree at Terrace Hill," Mrs. Tometich said. Other reminiscences by Nelson and Mrs. Tometich included:

- The interior of Terrace Hill. For instance, "Mrs. F.M. Hubbell's bedroom was a sight. She had lavender carpeting, lavender drapes, and with the white furniture and white marble fireplace, it was striking."
- Some of the goings-on outside the house. "The garage was used for the cars on the main floor and below when Dad was first there they had a family cow in the stable, and on the steeple they raised pigeons, as Mr. F.M. Hubbell was (mainly) a vegetarian and only ate squab which (was) raised for him. Attached to the garage was a little room used for Mary Belle's playhouse. After she tired of it, my sister and I were permitted to use it. We spent many a happy time in it." (The "little" room used for the playhouse was actually quite spacious. It had been used as the icehouse before the days of refrigerators. The ice was the sole means of keeping food cold. Hubbell employees would chop the ice from the Raccoon River, which ran conveniently close, south of Terrace Hill.)
- The renowned chandelier. "The chandelier in the main ballroom was a job that Dad and the housemen did not look forward to, as they had to remove each prism, wash and polish them, and return them to the chandelier. However, on party nights and at night, that was a sight to behold."

Despite the glamor associated with the mansion, F.M. Hubbell's years after his wife's death were not easy for him. He tried to be active, working at his office each day, even if all he did was to check the cash book. Every month he would leave Terrace Hill's confines to walk across the street to collect $20 from a garage worker who was buying property with Hubbell's financing. Hubbell's biographer said, "As age advanced, Hubbell's values inevitably changed. Railroads, banks, property, millions of dollars—all such things were not so important. What he wanted most of all now was for someone to come to see him, preferably his sons, grandsons or great-grandchildren. And he wanted Elmer Nelson, the family chauffeur, to take him riding, always on Avenue Frederick M. Hubbell. But Elmer frequently was too busy."

Hubbell was vitally interested in how long he would live. Part of his interest in life expectancy was probably tied to his actuarial concern with the profitabilty of Equitable Life Insurance Co. When recording the deaths of others in his diary, Hubbell

Chauffeur Elmer Nelson stands alongside Hubbell's 1909 eight-cylinder Cadillac. (Courtesy Frances Tometich.)

Elmer Nelson's home on Allen Place. Note the carriage house on the left and Terrace Hill on the right. (Courtesy Frances Tometich.)

often noted not only the person's age in years, but also calculated the number of months and days. In late 1924, Hubbell inquired about his own life expectancy. He was told by experts at Equitable that a man of eighty-six could expect to live another 3½ years. "If I do not reach the age of 89½ years, I shall not have had a fair count," Hubbell wrote. Although he prided himself on his good health, Hubbell spent much time confined to bed. In February 1926, he observed in his diary that he had not been outside of Terrace Hill for seventy-four days, commenting "I am awfully tired of it." He was able to communicate with the outside world more easily when in July 1929 the first dial telephone in Des Moines was installed at Terrace Hill. (As already noted, Hubbell in 1878 was the first Des Moines resident to have a telephone line between his office and home. But that was before he lived in Terrace Hill.)

One thing Hubbell did to keep busy was grant interviews to newspaper reporters who were fascinated with his wealth and longevity. One article, appearing the week of his ninetieth birthday in 1929, said, "Frederick Marion Hubbell will be

F. M. Hubbell mausoleum, Woodland Cemetery.

F. M. Hubbell's gold watch displayed in boardroom of the Hubbell Realty office.

ninety years old January 17. For Mr. Hubbell, it will be the customary birthday, but not the birthday customary to most people. Birthdays to most people are, in one respect, closely akin to Thanksgiving and Christmas. They call for a great deal of feasting —a generous helping of this and that. Not so for Mr. Hubbell. He regards overeating as mankind's deadliest foe. This birthday will mark the thirty-third year he has not partaken of meat except on rare occasions. 'To my light diet,' he once said, 'I owe my freedom from headache and illness.'" The article noted that Hubbell had much to look back on: "Having reached four score years and ten, Mr. Hubbell will probably find due cause for reflection as Thursday dawns. He may recall the days when Walnut Street ended in a wilderness at Sixth Avenue, when Grand Avenue was without automobiles and when his home was in the country . . . . For Mr. Hubbell, his ninetieth birthday will be another day of contrasts—Des Moines as it is now and Des Moines as it was sixty years ago when the youth who has now to be recognized as the state's wealthiest man was just developing the knack of picking up corner lots. Just lots they were then but 'sites' they afterwards became, and with their monetary growth, Mr. Hubbell grew. To the youth looking ahead, these ninety years seemed almost an indefinable lifetime. To a patriarch, such as Mr. Hubbell, they seem but a fleeting era. A fleeting era, and yet in that one span, Mr. Hubbell, perhaps more than any other Des Moines citizen, has distinguished himself in many fields."

After recounting Hubbell's successful business exploits, the article quoted his formula: "There are four requisites for financial success, and any man can amass a comfortable fortune with them. The first is economy. If a man spends all he makes, he can never be prosperous. The second is industry. No matter how talented he is, no man who is lazy can make financial progress. The third is good health. That is indispensable. With these three essentials, any man can accumulate $1,000 as a matter of course. The fourth essential is enough brains to invest that $1,000 and not lose it. Then his fortune is assured. That's all there is to making money."

Hubbell's life ended on November 11, 1930. He died, fittingly enough, at Terrace Hill. The Des Moines City Council held a special meeting to honor him, the Polk County Courthouse was closed in tribute, and various businesses shut down for a day. He was eulogized from many quarters. The *New York Times* considered the Midwestern tycoon important enough to publish an obituary. Almost everything Hubbell owned had been placed in his trust in 1903, or added to it later. His personal estate consisted of $500 for his membership in the Des Moines Club, $10 in cash, and $500 for his gold watch and goldheaded cane. His life insurance amounted to $18,133. Hubbell was buried at Woodland Cemetery in the family mausoleum. Hubbell was buried not far from B.F. Allen. Just as Terrace Hill had survived the death of its builder, so it would survive the death of its long-time patriarch. But it would do so amidst great controversy.

Chapter Twelve

Grover Carries On

With the death of F.M. Hubbell, Terrace Hill rightfully belonged to his eldest son Frederick C. to live in. But Frederick C. did not want to live there. Grover was already there with his family. So Grover stayed. He was to maintain residency with his wife Anna until his own death in 1956. Grover was forty-seven when his father died. Grover lived a full life, but did not make the newspapers nearly as much as F.M. or B.F. Allen, the first two masters of Terrace Hill. Grover was competent and successful, but in a quieter way. He spent his childhood and early adolescence in Des Moines. In 1898 he was sent to a military academy in Culver, Indiana. He went to prep school in Lawrenceville, New Jersey, and then to Yale University, where he received a degree in engineering in 1905. Later that year, he married Anna, the daughter of Des Moines pioneer George Godfrey. The ceremony was in the Godfrey home on Ninth Street. The bride was characterized as ''a young woman of exceptionally lovable qualities, and is a general favorite with all who know her. She has lived in Des Moines since childhood and was graduated from the West Des Moines High School in the class of 1902.'' The groom was termed ''a young man of ability and integrity and will be associated with his father and brother in managing their large business interests.''

In 1906, the Grover Hubbell family grew with the birth of daughter Frances. Helen (Virginia) was born in 1908 and Mary Belle in 1911. The family did not live in Terrace Hill at this time: the 1915 Census listed Grover's address as 2815 Ridge Road, and his occupation as ''real estate dealer.'' He was a trustee of Equitable Life Insurance and of his father's vast estate; treasurer or director of family-controlled firms such as Hubbell Realty Co., F.M. Hubbell, Son and Co., Hubbell Inc., and the Hubbell Building Co., plus vice-president of the Des Moines Terminal Co. and the Des Moines Western Railway Co. Grover was involved in ventures that did not have the Hubbell named attached, including the Angus Coal Co. in Oskaloosa, the Des Moines Elevator Co., Inland Mills Inc., and Valley Limestone and Gravel Co.

Grover's career was interrupted because of frail health. In 1918, his lung problems became so serious that the family moved to Los Alamos, New Mexico, and stayed for more than two years. Despite his ailments (he also suffered from arthritis),

Grover threw himself into community affairs when he returned to Des Moines. He was probably better known as a volunteer than as a businessman. In 1947, he was given the *Des Moines Tribune* Community Service Award. Among his positions noted by the judges were offices in the local YMCA and YWCA, president of the Drake University board of trustees, member of the Iowa Lutheran Hospital board of directors, plus affiliations with the Community Chest, Red Cross, Bureau of Municipal Research, Iowa Taxpayers Association, Salvation Army, and Boy Scouts. After learning of the award, Hubbell was characteristically humble: ''Whatever I have done in the way of community service has been done gladly and without any idea of seeking publicity,'' he said. ''I have gotten great satisfaction out of it. I feel that a man who has spare time owes some of it to the public. We all can show our appreciation of our American citizenship by performing some public service. What little I have been able to do has brought me much pleasure and many good friends.''

The hobbies of Grover Hubbell were well known to the public, making him seem less imposing than his father was. His stamp collection was valuable. Other avocations included baseball and deep sea fishing.

After everything about Grover's interests is said, though, what stands out was that he was senior trustee of the Hubbell estate. Managing the wealth so that it would be conserved was no small task. The estate held so much property that it was always involved in some transaction or controversy. In 1933 the estate trustees protested a city tax assessment of $2.5 million on seventy-six pieces of Hubbell-owned property. In the early 1950s the trustees, for the first time since the estate was established, asked for court permission to modify the terms. A modification was granted in 1952, allowing the trustees to invest in securities. The second modification, in 1954, allowed for the sale of forty-three acres along Avenue Frederick M. Hubbell.

Caring for the estate's assets meant caring for Terrace Hill. But Grover never believed the mansion had to be a lifeless place to be preserved. It was the scene of joyous occasions, as it had been in the days of B.F. Allen and F.M. Hubbell. Grover's daughter Helen Virginia was married there twice, in 1930 and 1942. Virginia's daughter Anne Weaver told the authors she remembered not only weddings at Terrace Hill, but also Christmas celebrations complete with roast suckling pig or a feast of roast goose raised on the grounds. In the summer Mah-jongg was played on the screened porch. Croquet was played on the back lawn around the pergola. Mrs. Weaver was married at Terrace Hill herself, in 1952. Grover's daughters Frances and Mary Belle had lavish receptions there after the wedding ceremonies. In 1955, Anna and Grover Hubbell celebrated their fiftieth wedding anniversary in the mansion with 300 guests.

The lavish parties were not the only reason Terrace Hill kept attracting attention. When novelist Edna Ferber was in

Pergola covered with wisteria, south lawn. (Drawing by S. Goettsch.)

Anne Thorne-Philip Weaver reception table, 1952. (Courtesy Anne Thorne Weaver.)

Anne Thorne-Philip Weaver wedding reception, 1952. (Courtesy Anne Thorne Weaver.)

Des Moines in 1933 visiting her friend Jay (Ding) Darling, whose own home had a view of Terrace Hill, she became fascinated with the mansion. In a novel published two years later under the title *Come and Get It,* Ferber used Terrace Hill as the model for a fictional mansion set in a small Wisconsin town. The book editor of the *Des Moines Register* noted the similarities. On the newspaper's book page, a passage from the novel ran alongside some photographs of Terrace Hill. Here is a part of the passage:

Down the stairway of his house came Barney Glasgow on his way to breakfast. A fine stairway, black walnut and white walnut. A fine house . . . . His fingertips just touched the banister. His eyes followed the flow of it. He thought it looked, with the morning light on it, like duck gravy, the patina of polish overlaying the dark wood like gleaming golden fat over meat stock. He came the length of the broad upper hall from either side of which the bedroom doors gave, in massive walnut dignity. In the exact center of the hall, which had the proportions of a large room, was a black walnut tete-a-tete chair, upholstered in crimson plush . . . . Then on, lightly, down the short flight of double stairs to the first landing. There his eye was gratified by the tapestry that all but covered the landing wall . . . . For it was a good tapestry, true in weave and dye. The brothers Gilles and Jean Gobelin themselves need not have blushed for it . . . . He descended the broad main flight that almost spanned the central lower hallway. The morning sunlight caught the prisms of the chandelier that hung there and shot them with orange and with ruby and emerald and aquamarine. Easterners, smug in their pride of early New England or late Victorian architecture, would have been astonished at the sight of this small-town Wisconsin house, and still more amazed to learn that it had stood thus in its handsome solidity of cream brick, cupolas, turrets, gazebo, stables, and boat house, for nearly half a century.

In 1941, city of Des Moines inspectors, also fascinated with the mansion, toured it. The house at that time carried a higher tax assessment than any other residence in Des Moines. The inspection report noted the heavy walnut and rosewood trim on the first and second floors, the ornate mahogany stairway, shutters on every window, ornate plaster ceilings, the high-grade interior finish, the elevator, six bathrooms of which one had marble wainscoting and three had ceramic tile floors and wainscoting, eight fireplaces, slate roof, and exterior walls of solid brick. Those walls were two feet thick. In 1948, the *Des Moines Register,* for no special reason except its interest in the mansion, published a picture-laden article. Of the staircase, the article said, ''The wide stair rail is in no danger of losing its high gloss, for Frederick Ingham (who was pictured)

and the five other grandsons of the present owners inevitably take the short-cut from the second to first floor, instead of using the elevator. Many sedate oldsters in Des Moines recall making flying entrances to the long hall below.'' The drawing room was described like this: ''Once the drawing room was bare, except for the gilt chairs brought in when the Hubbell women served chocolate to callers on their Tuesdays at home. Today the rock crystal chandelier shines on treasures garnered from many countries. At the left is a tapestry from Brussels and Chinese lanterns inlaid with melted buffalo horn; to the right is a Chinese hanging, whose five-toed dragons proclaim it was made for the Imperial Palace in Peking. There are Dresden jardinieres, a delicately wrought marble Ophelia from Italy, an etched brass coffee table from India, and a cabinet displaying Delft china from Holland, ivories, gem-studded ornaments, and figurines from around the world.''

The Hubbells traveled the world and brought back many possessions. Anna Hubbell sometimes returned with gifts for the household staff. She would buy them in quantity, such as a dozen pair of gloves or a dozen scarves. (While the Hubbells were traveling, the servants would cover the massive chandelier with thirty-six yards of muslin, said Carrie Larson of Des Moines, who visited head housekeeper Karina Rasmussen—her mother's first cousin—at the mansion. The muslin kept the chandelier clean, so that it did not have to be attended regularly.) The newspaper reporter toured the mansion with Anna Hubbell and described what she saw: ''Inside the front door are the canes in their rack exactly as the first owners would have wished to find them, the high hat rack, and the umbrella stand . . . . The accumulated oriental rugs, tapestries, oil portraits of several generations, objets d'art purchased on many trips abroad, the brass fireplace sets, needlepoint, tapestry and satin damask, upholstered chairs and sofas, the lamps, brocaded draperies— all belong to the rooms whose high ceilings have kept their fresco decorations. It does not seem rude to stare at the treasures amassed in Terrace Hill. In fact, the owners are happy to explain the sources of the huge temple bell with three-minute reverberations, the two-toned bronze Chinese water cooler held up on tusks of a teakwood stand, the Italian portrait painted on the great round blue porcelain plate . . . and the scores of other interesting appointments in the old home.'' Anna Hubbell told how she felt about the mansion: ''None of the family will be burdened with such a home. So we think of it as headquarters for our ten grandchildren, hoping they will retain the memory of many happy hours in the home of their great-grandparents.''

It seemed the public could not read enough about the mansion. A 1955 *Iowan* magazine article termed Terrace Hill ''undoubtedly the best-known house in Iowa.'' Little did the writer know that in two years the mansion would sit empty, except for caretakers. It should have been no surprise to an astute observer, however, that the house would not find an occupant among the Hubbells once Grover died. It was too impractical for a modern family. After Grover's death on December 9, 1956, he was lauded editorially for having "helped to keep traditions and memories of another era alive by arranging for the restoration of Terrace Hill." The editorial was on the mark—Terrace Hill indeed was of another era. Grover had lived nine years beyond the death of his elder brother Frederick C. Grover was soon followed in death by his sister Beulah and Frederick's sons Frederick W. and James. It was James' death in 1962 that triggered the countdown to the end of the Hubbell Trust.

Although the trust would end in 1983, that did not diminish the economic clout held by the Hubbells in Des Moines. The property of the trust, combined with the property of F.M. Hubbell, Son and Co. and the family's majority ownership of Equitable Life Insurance Co., added up to a vast fortune. Every year the trust made an accounting of its assets to the Polk County District Court. The accounting for the year ending June 30, 1977, showed the estate with assets of nearly $14 million, most of it invested in municipal bonds. The annual income topped $3 million, all from dividends and interest on the estate's investments. The estate had substantial holdings in the stock of affiliated companies, including 68 percent of Equitable Life. At the then current price on the stock market, those shares were worth close to $70 million. The estate also owned 80 percent of the common stock of F.M. Hubbell, Son and Co. Many of the Hubbell family holdings had been transferred from F.M.'s trust to F.M. Hubbell, Son and Co. There was good reason for what appeared to be mere shuffling of papers. The transfers, especially of real estate, gave the Hubbells more latitude to wheel and deal, since by law the trust had to be managed conservatively. F.M. Hubbell, Son and Co. did not operate under such restraints. Underneath the umbrella of F.M. Hubbell, Son and Co. were Hubbell Realty Co., engaged in land sales and management; Hubbell Development Co., engaged in land development; and the Des Moines Terminal Co., engaged in the leasing of railroad rights-of-way.

F.M. Hubbell's trust had preserved the family fortune for decades with little modification. But in the 1970s the trust underwent vast changes. The door to change was opened in 1969 when the trustees asked for court permission to sell the 132 pieces of Class A property that F.M. had designated as untouchable. (There were 108 pieces in 1903. The larger number resulted from several purchases, changes in platting, and the like.) Terrace Hill was specifically exempted from the request to the court. It was in a class by itself. The list of 132 parcels showed the dominance the family had over prime commercial land in Des Moines, especially in the downtown vicinity. Court permission was granted for the sale of the parcels. So the Hubbell estate began to splinter. But during all this, Terrace Hill—nearly deserted—stood majestically, a symbol of so much Iowa history. What would happen to the mansion?

Christmas, 1954 with Grover and Anna Hubbell, their ten grandchildren, and three great-grandchildren. (Courtesy Mary Belle Hubbell Windsor.)

Preliminary drawing for an engraving by Amy N. Worthen, commissioned by the trustees of the Terrace Hill Society.

Nineteenth century photograph of reception room where visitors were welcomed. (Courtesy William Wagner.)

Chapter Thirteen

A House
Is Not a Home

Although it was clear after Grover Hubbell's death that no other family member would want to live in Terrace Hill, there was no intention of abandoning what by then was called the "Hubbell mansion" as often as it was called Terrace Hill. In fact, just two months before Grover died, the trustees (including Grover) decided to rejuvenate the house by replacing woodwork, repairing the roof, and waterproofing the stone and brick masonry. The southeast fireplace stack was restored to working order, although three other stacks remained cemented shut. The work on the exterior alone cost $50,000.

There had been talk within the Hubbell family and outside it, too, that the mansion should be used for a public purpose. That talk intensified by mid-1957 after Anna, Grover's widow, moved out. The furniture, including pieces originally designed for the mansion, was distributed among third and fourth generation descendants. The house was closed. The Hubbells began discussions with the state of Iowa about a transfer of property. On August 14, 1957, Iowa Atty. Gen. Norman Erbe wrote a memorandum about a meeting with Phineas Henry, a lawyer representing the Hubbells. Two possible uses were discussed for Terrace Hill: making it part of the state Department of History and Archives, or using it as a governor's mansion. But if the state decided to accept the manion—for whatever use—it would be complicated, especially because of the considerable upkeep. Erbe noted three alternatives for the state to obtain it at a reasonable cost. The first was for the Hubbell trust to lease the house to the state for $1 a year. The trust would pay the real estate taxes, the state would absorb maintenance costs. The second alternative was for the state to acquire the property through friendly condemnation proceedings. The third was for the Hubbells to obtain court permission to break the 1903 trust and give the mansion to the state.

After Erbe's memorandum was written, Gov. Herschel Loveless and other state executives met with Hubbell trust representatives to discuss acquisition of Terrace Hill. Loveless decided the matter was one for the legislature, and appointed a ten-member committee to study the alternatives. In December 1957, the four senators and six representatives visited Terrace Hill, then met with Loveless and James W. Hubbell at the Capitol. The idea of converting the mansion to a governor's residence did not sit well with the committee. Loveless himself

was not pushing for it either, instead suggesting that a non-profit corporation operate Terrace Hill as a museum. For the next fifteen years, numerous interested parties had ideas about what to do with the mansion, but a consensus seemed impossible to reach.

The diversity of ideas was demonstrated at a meeting June 26, 1958, at the mansion. Represented were the Central Iowa Mineral Society, Des Moines Art Center, See Iowa First Club, Des Moines Founders Garden Club, National Society of Colonial Dames, Drake University, Des Moines City Council, Des Moines Register and Tribune Co., Des Moines Pioneer Club, Chamber of Commerce for Greater Des Moines, Iowa Department of History and Archives, The Questers, and the Iowa Society for the Preservation of Historic Landmarks. The meeting was organized by William Wagner, an architect with an interest in historic preservation. Before the meeting, he had visited the groups to ask, "If Terrace Hill were opened to the public, what use could your group make of the house?" Many answers were given. Dwight Kirsch of the Des Moines Art Center seemed to speak for some of those present when he said, "Having Terrace Hill open to the public for visits and conducted tours would greatly increase the cultural and study material in Des Moines. This mansion could serve as a museum house along with Salisbury House (another Des Moines mansion), in somewhat the same way as has been done with historic mansions in New York, Philadelphia, and elsewhere." Kirsch suggested that special exhibitions of antiques, tapestries, and other items be staged, with admission charged. Furnishings and art objects could be acquired for the mansion, to illustrate the decorative arts of the nineteenth century. But despite the enthusiasm generated by Kirsch's talk, nothing concrete resulted.

There was plenty of public support for opening the mansion, though. The Hubbell trust got letters constantly from groups around Iowa that wanted to tour the house. Simpson Smith, who ran the day-to-day operations of the Hubbell trust, was willing to open the house, but saw obstacles. In a letter dated October 2, 1957, Smith said, "I do hope that we can get under way and really accomplish something tangible. If we can ever find anyone who has an interest in Terrace Hill, then I will proceed to see what can be done insofar as the trustees of the Hubbell estate are concerned. I realize that the cost of operation is too high for most organizations. My thought is that if there is an interested party, I will ask the trustees if they would not subsidize the operation thereof by paying the taxes and the insurance coverage. The 1956 taxes payable in 1957 are $3,468. The insurance coverage is $1,010 per year. To give you an idea as to other operating costs during 1956, our gas bill was $1,245, the electricity $389, the water $269. I would also suggest to the trustees that we complete the exterior rehabilitation. With that work already done, together with the rehabilitation of the masonry, the mansion should stand without any depreciable exterior repairs for the next twenty-five or thirty-five years.''

Although little progress was being made to assure the mansion's long-term existence, Terrace Hill partisans were buoyed by the ''discovery'' in 1959 that the architect of the house had been William W. Boyington. The announcement was made by current-day architect Wagner, who said the information had been found during a systematic search of old newspapers. Despite some scholarly opinion that Boyington was more prolific than talented, Terrace Hill lovers were having none of it. ''He was a highly important man of his time, and Des Moines is fortunate to have Terrace Hill, a masterpiece of his style,'' Wagner said. Soon thereafter, the Iowa Society for Preservation of Historic Landmarks was incorporated to sponsor a campaign to save the mansion.

Through all this, the house remained closed to the curious, with only a few privileged groups allowed inside. In 1959 a gathering of Equitable Life Insurance Co. agents from across the nation received a tour. Response to the occasional viewings was so positive that in 1960 the Hubbell trustees started to assemble furniture from the mid and late 1800s to help some of the rooms come alive. The drawing room was refurnished with Victorian objects from the Cyrus B. Hillis residence in Des Moines. Pieces of marble statuary from Terrace Hill's original furnishings were retrieved and placed in the drawing room. The floor-to-ceiling mirror in that room was always impressive. A few other rooms were partially furnished, and some period floor coverings were laid. Late in that year, the mansion was opened to Equitable Life employees for a day. Company president James Windsor and his wife Mary Belle Hubbell Windsor showed the visitors the rooms where she had once lived. But the house's future remained in doubt, despite such brief rays of hope. The magazine for Equitable Life's home office employees published an article that asked ''What will become of Terrace Hill?'' The answer was indefinite, bordering on gloom. For what group would be willing to take over the annual tax bill topping $4,000 and the annual maintenance bill averaging $15,000?

Throughout the 1960s, that was the pattern: Everybody who thought about Terrace Hill wanted it saved, and almost everybody had an idea about how it should be used. But nobody would make a commitment. There was plenty of ballyhoo, however. A major New York publisher issued a book called *Great Houses of America,* in which Terrace Hill was listed with such notable mansions as Thomas Jefferson's Monticello and William Randolph Hearst's La Casa Grande. In 1967 the Hubbell family satisfied some of the curiosity about Terrace Hill by publishing a booklet in conjunction with the one-hundredth birthday of Equitable Life. The booklet, noting that the Hubbell trust ''has continued the careful maintenance of the buildings and grounds,'' said of the mansion's condition: ''After almost 100 years of exposure to Iowa's weather, the stone and brick exterior is sound, the rafters and joists are firm. The walls

which were paneled, papered or painted in ornate patterns, and the ceilings intricately molded and richly illuminated in gold and silver and color, have faded through the passage of time. The elaborate combinations of woodwork which enhance the interior beauty of Terrace Hill can still be seen.'' The booklet contained a brief description of each of the main rooms, presenting a verbal picture for those who had never been inside. The description that follows was put together from the booklet, material written the same year by Simpson Smith, and from other sources:

•Entrance hall and north hall: The chain in the hallway had been installed to hold back guests on evenings when open houses were held. The hall tree was an original, as were the gas ceiling lights converted to electricity when Grover Hubbell moved into the house.

•East hall: The massive hall tree was built for the mansion, and was standing where it had been originally placed. It had a pink marble base matched by pink marble tops and bases for the radiators. The moose, caribou, and elk heads—typical Victorian trophies—were shot by the Hubbells. The picture of Frederick C. Hubbell at about age ten was painted by an itinerant artist.

•West hall: This had been the music room, where a large square Chickering piano stood. The music room was eliminated in 1924 to make way for a powder room, an elevator, a closet, and a hallway to the outside garage that had been added to the house.

•Drawing room: The double doors were twelve feet high at their peaks, made of solid walnut with burl panels 3¼ inches thick, silver plate hardware, and cover plate hinges. The original items in the room were the Italian marble fireplace, rosewood mantel mirror, and matching pier mirror. The chandelier had been hung in 1884, soon after Hubbell bought the mansion from Allen. The shutters and sash were walnut. The Renaissance tapestry belonged to Grover and Anna Hubbell. The room, with its fifteen-foot ceilings, was the focal point of the home's famous society evenings.

•Reception room: The fireplace and walnut mantel mirror were prominent in this room. The two paintings were Italian, the vase was Meissen. The doors, ceilings, paneling, and trim were a combination of walnut and burl walnut woods.

•Living room: The fireplace was the only one of the eight original fireplaces that still worked. The three chairs probably were designed for the house. They had been found in the attic and restored. The sliding doors were in good working order. This had been the family area of Terrace Hill. It was Grover's favorite room because it was light and had a good view outside. The room had six windows, providing views to the north, east, south, and southwest.

•Library: The three corner pictures were of F.M. Hubbell, Frances Cooper Hubbell, and her father Isaac Cooper. The light fixtures contained opal-like stones. The bookcases were

Library.

Library.

Nineteenth century photographs of Terrace Hill interior. (Courtesy William Wagner.)

enclosed with French glass. The Oriental vase was a long-time decoration.

•Dining room: The semicircular bay was where the Hubbell family had dined together. The rest of the room was generally not used for meals unless guests were present. The egg and dart molding on the huge built-in sideboard were the Greek symbols for life and death. The grape leaf on the wainscot and the white oak detail were handcarved.

•Pantry: Indications are that the kitchen was not in the main house when Allen built Terrace Hill, although an 1867 newspaper article describing the plans for the mansion did place the kitchen within. It was common for kitchens of gentry homes to remain separate from the actual living quarters. There was less risk of the residence being destroyed by a kitchen fire. The black cast-iron stoves often used for cooking were regarded with suspicion for many decades because people feared explosions, poisoning, or gas-flavored food. Hubbell eventually moved the kitchen to the basement of the main house, according to Simpson Smith. A dumbwaiter connected it to the pantry directly above. Once the food was lifted to the pantry, it was taken from the dumbwaiter and placed on trays in a warming oven which had steam pipes circulating throughout. This allowed the food to remain hot until the servants were called to serve the meal.

•Rear stairway: Adjacent to the pantry was the servants' rear stairway, which led down to the kitchen and up to the second and third floors. The stairway was strictly utilitarian—narrow and winding, drab, it was not at all a match for the grand stair. After using the rear stairs to arrive on the third floor, one could walk a couple of steps to an unusual bridge (or walkway) that led into a small room. The narrow bridge was open on both sides, except for a railing allowing one to look below into the stair which it crisscrossed. At one time a reservoir for drinking water had been located in the small room. Water was pumped to a tank and fed by gravity to the house. It was used for other purposes, too. Mary Belle Hubbell Windsor recalled she was told that her father Grover and his first cousin Fred Thompson were caught swimming in it while they were boys. They received stern punishment for their transgression, she said.

•South hall and grand stairway: The staircase was made of oak, with balusters and rails of walnut and oak, and handrails of highly polished rosewood. The panels in the wainscot were cherry. One of the four corner closets concealed firefighting equipment and a clothes chute. That closet had originally housed a one-person hand-operated elevator. Evidence of its existence was the round glass inserts in the door, a feature absent from the other closets.

•Old bathroom: This may have been the only bath existing in the 1960s that dated back to Allen's occupancy, although a newspaper account predating the construction of Terrace Hill casts some doubt on there being just one bath in Allen's mansion. Features included a porcelain tub, lavatory, and marble floors.

Northeast bedroom.

Northwest bedroom.

Southeast master bedroom suite.

Nineteenth century photographs of Terrace Hill interior. (Courtesy William Wagner.)

• Bedrooms: The northeast bedroom belonged to F.M. Hubbell after his wife Frances died in 1924. The furniture for the most part had originally been in the master bedroom, including the bed and dresser. The bookshelves, though, had been specifically built for the northeast bedroom. The master, or southeast, bedroom, had belonged to Anna and Grover Hubbell after the death of Frances. It was part of a suite that included a sitting room, dressing room, and bath. The fireplace in the bedroom, of Italian marble, was original to the house. The bay window looked out over the Raccoon River to the wooded area that became Water Works Park. The northwest bedroom had been occupied by Beulah Hubbell before her marrige. Anna Hubbell took the brass bed from this room with her when she moved from Terrace Hill. The southwest bedroom contained a Victorian bed and dresser of the design popularized by Charles Lock Eastlake. The pieces were shipped from New York City in the late 1860s.

• Tower: The ninety-foot tower was on the north point of the house. There was a secondary turret on the east side portion. As a child, Mary Belle Hubbell and her friends used a ladder to climb into the top of the smaller turret. One day while they were playing up there, a male servant entered the bathroom below to wash himself. The girls' curiosity got the best of them, and they spied on the man. They might have gone undetected, but their giggles and dust falling from the trap door gave them away. Grover learned of the incident, reprimanded his daughter and closed the hole that allowed her access into the turret. Within the main tower was a storage vault on the lower level, a vestibule leading to the main hall on the first floor, an office-sewing room combination on the second floor, and a winding stair on the third-floor level that climbed nearly to the top of the tower. The walnut stair rail and balustrade led to a small landing from which one could continue to the uppermost part of the tower using a sharply pitched ladder, or pass through arched windows onto a bracketed balcony girdling the tower. This was a good spot for surveying surrounding vistas.

Although Terrace Hill was abandoned, it continued to amaze viewers. A Hollywood producer, seeing it for the first time, decided he had to shoot some scenes from the movie *Cold Turkey* there. Because the film was set in North Carolina, there were difficulties to overcome, but the producer was insistent. Despite all the interest, there were disquieting rumors that the mansion would be torn down. Supporters were discouraged at the Hubbell trust's inability to find an occupant. But, just about that time, some state legislators renewed the idea of converting Terrace Hill into a mansion for the governor, an idea that had been quashed in the late 1950s. State Rep. William Darrington, a member of the Capitol Planning Commission, said he liked the idea. The then current governor's mansion, six blocks to the west of Terrace Hill, had many drawbacks, he said. In early 1970, a subcommittee of Iowa House members was named to look at the possibility of acquiring Terrace Hill. Rep. William Winkelman, who made the subcommittee appointments, said, ''I feel strongly that we should be concerned about the preservation of this magnificent nineteenth century Iowa mansion. It is a meaningful symbol of the great traditions of our state. Pride in our traditions is an important factor in our state development. I hope we can get the general public behind us on this.'' A few weeks later, several legislators introduced a bill to give the Iowa Executive Council (consisting of the governor and other elected officials) the authority to acquire Terrace Hill if the Hubbell family were willing. One sponsor, Sen. Charlene Conklin, said the mansion might be destroyed unless action were taken to save it, and soon. When the 1970 legislature adjourned, the Executive Council had the authority to begin negotiations.

Why had the restoration of Terrace Hill suddenly become popular among legislators? Iowa Treasurer Maurice Baringer said during a 1978 interview with the authors that legislators realized the need to replace the mansion at 2900 Grand Avenue was more pressing than before. Although there was support to build a brand-new governor's home on the Capitol grounds, acquiring Terrace Hill seemed more sensible. That way, the first family would have a spacious residence, and a historic site would be saved from possible destruction. Governor Ray and his wife Billie shared that feeling. ''If a new governor's home had been built . . . . Terrace Hill would have become a cold museum, because most people would still want to visit the governor's home regardless,'' Mrs. Ray maintained later. That the Rays were inclined toward holding social functions probably influenced their efforts on behalf of a larger mansion. Gov. Harold Hughes, Ray's predecessor, had not been one for social gatherings.

Architect William Wagner in an interview with the authors mentioned other causes. ''There wasn't much appreciation of Terrace Hill back in the 1950s,'' he said. ''By the late 1960s, Victorian architecture had come of age. The building was put on the National Register of Historic Places, experts praised it, and so awareness increased.'' A vital part was played by the Hubbell family. ''There was a reversal of our stance that we'd sell it,'' said James W. Hubbell, Jr., the family's spokesman. ''Instead, we began thinking we'd donate it.''

While support was growing for a state takeover of Terrace Hill, the Hubbell trust issued a list of ''major repairs'' to the house from 1949 through 1969. The total cost was $98,200. That amount did not include money spent for normal upkeep. Perhaps one reason for the list was to demonstrate that the Hubbells had not let the mansion deteriorate extensively, as some critics were hinting. The largest amounts had been spent like this: a new boiler and water heater, $5,000 in 1949; replacement of windows, trim, and railings on the tower and dormers, $16,000 in 1957; painting of exterior trim, $4,000 in 1957; pruning and trimming trees, $5,000 in 1959; restoring masonry on exterior walls, $12,000 in 1960; restoring

the exterior of the carriage house and reshingling the roof with cedar shingles, $16,000 in 1964; removing diseased elm trees, almost $9,000 in the last half of the 1960s.

Support for acquiring Terrace Hill as a governor's mansion was building in places besides the legislature. In May 1970, the Polk County Historical Society met to discuss Terrace Hill's future. Speakers at the meeting sought to defuse any opposition to conversion as a governor's mansion by contending the cost would be not be high. A tentative architectural plan was presented by LeRoy Pratt, who was active in historic preservation around Iowa. Pratt's plan, conceived largely by architect Wagner, called for the first floor of Terrace Hill to be used for receptions. It would also be open for public tours, much like the White House. The second floor would contain executive offices, two sitting rooms, a dining room, and a kitchen. The third floor would be for sleeping. The cost of this would be about $150,000, historical society members were told. Another speaker at the meeting said she had met with the Rays and reported that the couple was enthusiastic about the proposed conversion. The speaker noted that other states were spending much more than $150,000 to build new homes for their governors.

One reason for the Rays' enthusiasm was what they felt to be the inadequacies of 2900 Grand Avenue. ''It was hard to avoid public scrutiny there,'' Billie Ray said in a 1978 interview with the authors. ''The security guards and the household help were there, almost living with us. If we had a sick child, she couldn't just get up and go to the kitchen in her nightgown, because there was no telling who would see her.'' Mrs. Ray said when guests arrived early, she could not get to her downstairs clothes closet without embarrassment. There was only the front entrance to the house, which meant it was sometimes impossible for the governor to avoid visitors when entering. Mrs. Ray remembered one instance when, upon stopping at the mansion to change clothes before a meeting, Governor Ray encountered 500 girl scouts on the main floor. Many wanted his autograph. He signed, making him late for the meeting.

The house at 2900 Grand Avenue had seemed like a good buy in 1947 when the state purchased it from Gerard Nollen, then chairman of the Bankers Life Insurance Company. The house was built in 1903 by W.W. Witmer and had remained in the family, as Mrs. Nollen was Witmer's daughter. The state had paid $27,200 for the home and its 240-foot by 200-foot lot. The remodeling needed for conversion to a governor's mansion cost another $23,000, with $22,000 more spent on furnishings. Buying the home was controversial because it was not an Iowa tradition to supply a house for the governor. The only governor to live in a state-owned residence was William Harding, from 1917 to 1921. The house was at 1027 Des Moines Street, a few blocks from the Capitol. Otherwise, Iowa governors had to fend for themselves. Gov. William Beardsley was the first Iowa governor to reside at 2900 Grand, moving there in early 1949. Although the house was never as opulent as Terrace Hill, and although it was not well-designed for a first family, it was nothing to sneer at. When a visitor entered, he was greeted by a colonial staircase with a mahogany handrail and white balustrade. The woodwork was oak in the drawing room and the library. The downstairs also contained two dining rooms, a kitchen, and a screened porch. On the second floor were five bedrooms and a sitting room. There were four baths in the house, plus two rooms on the top floor used as servants' quarters.

The Rays were looking forward to someday moving to Terrace Hill, and things started falling into place in 1971. The Hubbells offered the mansion to the state, with only minimal conditions attached. The state would have to preserve the house for at least twenty-five years, retain the name "Terrace Hill," and install a plaque listing names of donors. Governor Ray praised the eight Hubbell heirs for offering the mansion with so few conditions. He reiterated that it should become a governor's home, with parts open for public tours. The House and Senate overwhelmingly approved authorizing the state to accept the Hubbells' gift. Rep. Don Alt, chairman of the committee handling the acquisition, said how the mansion would be used was for the 1972 Iowa General Assembly to decide. There was no guarantee that Terrace Hill would become a governor's home. One reservation among legislators was that public access to a governor's home would necessarily be limited; yet there was obviously public interest in touring Terrace Hill. That was

Hubbell family members present August 24, 1971. They officially gave the key to Terrace Hill to Iowa Gov. Robert Ray. (Courtesy Mary Belle Hubbell Windsor.)

why several members said they might push an alternative plan in the 1972 session—building a separate governor's residence on the eight-acre Terrace Hill grounds. Terrace Hill itself would be a museum, with daily visiting hours. The governor could use it for official functions, especially large social gatherings. Representative Alt said that plan would mean a more faithful restoration, since Terrace Hill would not have to be modified for use as living quarters. Iowa Secretary of State Melvin Synhorst, a member of the powerful Executive Council, told the authors in a 1978 interview that he had questions about the fidelity of restoration from the beginning. Synhorst said he finally voted for turning Terrace Hill into a governor's home, but only reluctantly.

The Hubbell trust carried out its obligation by obtaining permission in Polk County District Court to alter the 1903 document so that Terrace Hill could be given to the state. The judge noted "significant changes of circumstances" since 1903, including:

•Life-style changes which made the huge nineteenth century home unsuitable as a twentieth century residence for most families.

•Changes in technology which required substantial outlays for the installation of modern home conveniences.

•Changes in land use in the Terrace Hill neighborhood.

•The decision by F.M. Hubbell's heirs not to occupy the mansion, which meant it would probably remain unoccupied until the trust expired in 1983.

•Expenses that the trust would incur to maintain an unoccupied house. The total was estimated at a minimum of $260,000 for the twelve years then remaining in the life of the trust.

With legal obstacles removed, the mansion was formally presented to the state on August 24, 1971, at a ceremony outside the house on the south lawn. Four generations of the Hubbell family—including Anna Hubbell, the last occupant—watched as James W. Hubbell, Jr. gave the keys to Governor Ray. The Hubbell heirs went in debt $263,000 to give the house away. The conveyance had to be paid for by somebody, because it was a Hubbell trust asset. Future heirs had to be compensated in some way. The $263,000 price was approved by the court as reasonable. The replacement cost of the mansion and its contents was many times higher, but the "fair market value" almost certainly was not. After all, in the 1970s who would buy such a house, with its tremendous bills for upkeep alone? The Hubbell trust eased the burden on the eight family members absorbing the debt by allowing repayment of the $263,000 principal to be deferred until 1983. Notes were issued to the eight family members at 6 percent interest.

But that was no affair of the state. It had gained possession of Terrace Hill, the home that had passed from B.F. Allen to F.M. Hubbell to Grover Hubbell, and that for nearly fifteen years had been lived in only by caretakers. Now the question was, what to do with the symbolic mansion, and how to do it?

Chapter Fourteen

Enter the State

One of the first things the state did was to conduct an inventory of everything that remained inside Terrace Hill. Some items of the hundreds on the list included clothing of ancient vintage found in a wardrobe (a beaver top hat of F.M. Hubbell's, a black beaded cape with matching handbag, and beaded white kid party pumps); a hall tree with a leather seat and a mirror; library sets, such as twenty-five volumes of George Eliot's writings, and twenty-three volumes of Robert Louis Stevenson's works; part of the first set of dishes owned by F.M. and Frances Hubbell; a wooden baby buggy; a dollhouse; ice skates; a carved sofa; a large late Victorian bed with matching dresser; a croquet set; and about 150 fruit jars. There were also four elaborate tapestries, one dating to the 1500s.

The state self-insured the mansion, rather than retaining the $750,000 worth of insurance that the Hubbell trust had been carrying. Many items had been insured separately. The stained glass window on the second floor landing was insured for $7,500.

The most significant early step taken to determine the mansion's future came on November 15, 1971, when Governor Ray appointed the thirty-five member Terrace Hill Planning Commission. Its purpose was to develop recommendations for the use of Terrace Hill. The chairman was George Mills, the authorized biographer of F.M. Hubbell and a veteran political reporter for the *Des Moines Register.* Named to the group's executive committee were State Sen. Charlene Conklin, Secretary of State Synhorst, Coon Rapids banker John Chrystal, West Des Moines lawyer John Ward, architect Wagner, librarian Elaine Estes, magazine editor Terrance Elsberry, and Billie Ray. The first commission secretary was Scherrie Goettsch, one of the authors of this book. Governor Ray said he appointed such a potentially unwieldy number of people because ''I felt we needed people participation to get the word out, to get citizens interested because the commission members became enchanted on their own.'' Synhorst was critical of the commission. ''It was a great democratic exercise and a broad range of interests were represented, but it wasn't efficient,'' he said in a 1978 interview. ''We probably needed a single person to direct the whole project. There have been so many cooks involved that the broth was spoiled. A committee can't paint a work of art, and Terrace Hill is a work of art.'' Some critics said that the Terrace Hill Planning Commission did have

a single director, in fact if not in name: Billie Ray. The critics said the governor had stacked the deck so that the commission would recommend use of Terrace Hill as a governor's home. Within ten weeks, the group presented its recommendations to the legislature. It suggested the best use would be as a governor's home. The ten recommendations, made public on February 3, 1972, were as follows:

1. That the third floor of Terrace Hill be converted into official living quarters for Iowa's governor and family. The second floor would be used for guest rooms and study area for the governor and spouse. The original architecture of the second floor would remain practically unchanged. The first or main floor would remain practically as is, except for decorating modifications. Members of the commission, during inspections of the building, observed that the third floor of the mansion was originally an open ballroom of clear-span design. It was subsequently partitioned into smaller rooms as living quarters for servants and for storage. It was the opinion of the commission that remodeling this area into suitable quarters for habitation by a family would not disrupt either the historical or architectural integrity of Terrace Hill. *(This recommendation, like some of the others, was controversial. Many experts believed the third floor had never been a ballroom. Architect Wagner was one of those experts. But his associate Lawrence Ericsson thought it likely that the third floor had indeed been a ballroom. Wagner and Ericsson agreed, however, that the planning commission's conclusion was based on little hard evidence.)*

2. That funds other than those appropriated by the General Assembly for the restoration and preservation of Terrace Hill be raised by any or all of the following procedures—fund-raising occasions such as dinners, sale of commemorative medallions, and acceptance of gifts, including those from private foundations, federal grants, and all other sources, plus any other legitimate means.

3. That provision be made for regular public tours through Terrace Hill, with appropriate literature, tour guides, and safety precautions.

4. That the public be encouraged to donate art objects, furniture, paintings, etcetera, compatible with the structure.

5. That appropriate professional personnel be employed to plan all proposed changes.

6. That adequate parking facilities be established.

7. That safeguards be established to insure that the land and buildings which comprise Terrace Hill be preserved basically as is for the benefit of posterity. This could be accomplished through the creation of a statutory, non-partisan committee with final authority

over all decisions made relative to Terrace Hill.

8. That the present governor's residence, located at 2900 Grand Avenue in Des Moines, be sold, with the proceeds of such sale to be applied to the restoration and preservation of Terrace Hill.

9. That legislation be enacted by the General Assembly, where necessary, to implement the recommendations contained in this report.

10. That funding be provided by the General Assembly to carry out the commission recommendations where other sources for funding will not be adequate.

Some people were skeptical of the commission's report. State Rep. Norman Rodgers said Terrace Hill might lose its Victorian flavor if converted to a governor's home. It was not only the security system that would have to be maintained, or the public restrooms that would have to be provided. ''How are antiques going to survive if they are going to be used for everyday living?'' Rodgers asked. ''Most of our recent governors have had growing children. (The Rays had three daughters.) How are you going to confine them to the third floor? Have you ever tried to confine your children to any one level of your home for any length of time?'' But in general, the commission recommendations were not controversial. State Rep. Keith Dunton estimated the governor could be living at Terrace Hill within two years. The Polk County Historical Society echoed that estimate in its newsletter, mentioning a conversion cost of $250,000. How wrong they would be!

That cost estimate bedeviled Terrace Hill supporters in later years. Stanley McCausland, head of the Iowa Department of General Services, told the authors in a 1978 interview that in 1972, he thought the $250,000 was reasonably accurate. It did not take him long to realize it was too low. But, he said, ''We were stuck with that public estimate. We were stuck with that posture.'' Yet then, in early 1972, there was cause for optimism. In March, the General Assembly approved converting Terrace Hill to a governor's home. The Executive Council was given day-to-day supervisory powers and told by the legislators to make ''the first floor of Terrace Hill available to the public, subject to reasonable restrictions in order to preserve its primary function for use by the governor for offical state functions, and in order to preserve the beauty, decor, and antiquity.'' The Executive Council was authorized to accept gifts and federal funds for Terrace Hill. The legislators, however, did not appropriate any money for the project. That did not bother State Treasurer Baringer at the time—he hoped to raise money privately, steering clear of a body which he felt had a poor track record when it came to granting funds for historic preservation. (In later years, when private fund-raising efforts were lagging, Baringer wished the legislature had been more generous.)

On April 18, 1972, Governor Ray signed the legislature's bill, even though sources of money were undefined. The governor said: ''Ahead lies a statewide effort to raise the necessary funds to bring the building into suitable condition to open it to the public for regularly scheduled tours, to enhance the surrounding grounds, and to convert the upper floor of the mansion to modern living quarters.'' But, said the governor—noting ''the exceptional interest in this historic home among Iowans in all walks of life''—it would be only ''a matter of time'' before the project would be completed. A ''matter of time'' was an indefinite phrase, of course, but not even the most pessimistic observers thought that six years later, the mansion would still be closed to a curious public.

As the mansion passed to the state, it was the subject of feature treatments in Iowa newspapers, magazines, and business publications. Terrace Hill became the symbol of Iowa to out-of-state residents. The mansion was nominated for the National Register of Historic Places. The nomination, submitted to the National Park Service, listed the physical condition as ''good.'' It said that ''several persons who should know have stated that Terrace Hill is the finest piece of Victorian architecture between Chicago and California. Earl Reed, who was national chairman of the American Institute of Architects' committee on preservation, said, 'Contrary to all other Victorian mansions that I have seen, Terrace Hill's woodwork is all solid wood, no graining was used on the first or second floors, the eight fireplaces are real, the detail is all in such perfect scale with the unusally large rooms and halls that one is misled as to the size of the rooms.''

But all the praise did not start the dollars flowing for restoration and renovation. As a result, in June 1972 an organi-

Long lines at state's first official open house, held on four Sunday afternoons in 1972.

zation calling itself the Terrace Hill Society was incorporated to raise funds. The incorporators were George Mills, John Chrystal, and John Ward, all influential members of the Terrace Hill Planning Commission, plus State Treasurer Baringer. Their fund-raising task did not seem difficult, given the oft-quoted estimate that the work would not cost over $250,000. To heighten interest with the public, the mansion was opened during four Sundays in September and October 1972. The response was overwhelming. People had to wait in line for hours, and each week some had to be turned away. The total topped 12,000. No admission was charged. In the program handed to visitors, however, the Terrace Hill Society solicited ''finely crafted furniture and accessories of the nineteenth century.'' And visitors were advised that donations of money would be tax deductible. Only $728 was donated on the spot; another $710 came from the sale of Terrace Hill postcards, notecards and watercolors.

Money did not begin to flow from the public until December 1972, when the Terrace Hill Society sold silver and bronze medallions imprinted with replicas of the mansion. The sales

Vaulted brick tunnel connecting Terrace Hill and the carriage house. (Courtesy Lawrence Ericsson.)

were made at about 600 Iowa banks. Untold thousands of dollars in sales were lost, however, by poor planning. The first minting of 33,000 medallions was exhausted before Christmas, leaving an unmet demand among people who wanted to give the mementos as holiday gifts. Another 35,000 were struck at the Franklin Mint in Philadelphia, but it was too late. The sales surge was never duplicated. By mid-1973, sales totals were 12,300 silver medallions and 32,600 bronze medallions. That was fewer than had been anticipated, which hurt the Terrace Hill fund-raising effort greatly because the sales were profitable.

Because little money was available, the Executive Council dug into its discretionary accounts and found $25,000 for work on the mansion's carriage house. An apartment was to be constructed there for caretakers. Rooms would be made into a museum display area and a security office. The rooms had originally been used as a carriage garage, tack room, and an icehouse. The project also would move the heating system away from the mansion to the carriage house basement, where it had been in B.F. Allen's day. As with so many other Terrace Hill plans, this one went awry. When the bids were opened, they were way above the cost estimate. The Executive Council rejected them, deciding instead to scale down the carriage house project. But nothing was done for years. The work on the third floor by that time carried an estimated cost of $448,000. A private entrance would be built after removal of the garage that the Hubbells had added. Architect Wagner said he expected work on the third floor to begin in June 1973, with the governor moving in about a year later. The Iowa House approved a $450,000 appropriation during 1973 to cover much of the third floor renovation, but the Senate would not go along. The General Assembly adjourned without appropriating a penny for Terrace Hill.

It was not a time of unbroken doom for the project, however. Terrace Hill was approved for inclusion on the National Register of Historic Places, making it eligible for federal funding. Also, as workers started going over the house and grounds, some forgotten features were stumbled upon. One was a long-hidden steam tunnel, found when a stove in the mansion's basement was moved. The other end of the tunnel had previously been uncovered in the carriage house. Since the mansion was originally heated by fireplaces, the tunnel may have been a later addition. Later, underneath the basement's concrete slab floor, a network of much smaller brick-vaulted tunnels was found. The architects surmised that the network was part of a warm air heating system. Mary Belle Hubbell Windsor told the authors that she remembered playing in the large tunnel leading to the carriage house as a child, proving it had not been entirely unknown. Mrs. Windsor recalled crawling into the tunnel one day with some girl friends, without parental permission. The girls took food with them in order to snack while exploring. But they had to turn back when the tunnel narrowed at a manhole where perhaps a windmill had once sat aboveground. Wagner hailed the uncovering of the entrance, saying the

Roof renovation required extensive scaffolding in late 1974.

Scaffolding surrounds west garage, which was removed for music room renovation.

tunnel could be used for steam pipes and utility lines. Later in 1973, the mansion's original boiler room and coal storage area were found underground. That discovery was expected to make reopening of the steam tunnel easier.

As the 1974 legislature convened, Terrace Hill supporters were optimistic that money would be forthcoming. Private fund raising was not working. At the very least, it was hoped the Senate would go along with the House's $450,000 appropriation of the previous year. But the Senate was not ready to be that generous. In fact, for awhile it appeared there would be no money appropriated in 1974 because of opposition to the entire project among some legislators. State Sen. Elizabeth Shaw, who chaired a key appropriations subcommittee, disliked the idea of Terrace Hill as a governor's home. State Rep. James Caffrey said he was delighted with the Senate's intransigence. He called the mansion ''Termite Hill,'' contending that the house was riddled with structural defects. But the opposition was partially overcome. When the 1974 session was over, the Executive Council had $200,000 from the legislature. The council moved immediately to fix the mansion's leaking roof. The estimated cost was $40,000; the low bid came in at $98,000! The council awarded the contract anyway because the leaking was so serious. But nobody was predicting anymore that Governor Ray would be calling the mansion home in 1974. Mid-1975 became the target date.

Money was so scarce that there was serious talk of melting down the 15,000 unsold silver medallions. It was estimated that such a measure would net $75,000. That would have helped, but it was far short of the $225,000 that would have resulted if the medallions had been sold. There were also about 40,000 unsold bronze medallions. George Mills, who had stepped down as chairman of the Terrace Hill Planning Commission but who retained close ties to the project, wrote in July 1974 that the plans for Terrace Hill would have to be scaled down: ''Because all the needed money is not yet available, and because of soaring costs, some of the planned improvements and restorations are being put off for a few years. The present boiler, which has been giving satisfactory service, will not now be replaced. Nor will the tunnel leading to the carriage house be rebuilt. The ultimate plan is to locate a new boiler at its original site adjoining the carriage house and to rebuild the tunnel, which first will be used to transmit air conditioning from compressors at the carriage house. The back stairway in Terrace Hill will be left intact, not rebuilt now as had been planned. Nor will the main kitchen in the basement be redone for the present. And not as much air conditioning will be installed as planned at first.''

Architect Wagner, writing for a professional magazine in the autumn of 1974, was worried about his plans being sabotaged by lack of money. He complained that the working drawings had been done for over a year, but lay collecting dust. The roof was deteriorating rapidly, causing damage to the ornate plaster of the second floor ceiling. Moisture had penetrated

Terrace Hill, late 1974.

Architect William Wagner at job site; Governor's private entrance is under construction.

to the first floor ceiling, too. A tin roof for the porch had to be delayed because no money was available. Other roofing plans were cut back. The rough paint on the mansard roof and its cornice was scraped, rather than removed entirely. Because of safety regulations, scaffolding had to be erected, adding an unexpected $11,000 to the cost. "When the roof costs went so high," Wagner wrote, "it was decided to provide a realistic cost take-off for the balance of the restoration and rehabilitation. This figure has not been officially released. But the general contract work was approximately as much as the entire original estimate for all trades. Because of inflated costs, there is currently a revised scheme for restoration. Less ambitious, this provides for restoration and a minimum of structural change to the third floor, where the governor's living quarters will be. The last legislative session appropriated $200,000 for redoing the mechanical services in the mansion. This mechanical work needs to be completed—but there needs to be some general work accomplished at the same time. Whatever gets done will hopefully not change the original plan." Wagner's article did mention some bright spots. Restoration had been completed on the two towers, mansard roof, upper and lower gutters, main hip roof, and main cornice at the bottom of the mansard. The original paint color had been discovered. It was a heavy gold paint that had ground-up nutshells added to it.

Although the Terrace Hill project had been plagued by inefficiency from the start, skeptics who were beginning to wonder if the whole effort had turned into a boondoggle were reluctant to speak out. Terrace Hill was a symbol of pride to many Iowans. So the enthusiasts continued to get their way more often than not. The Terrace Hill Planning Commission's furnishings committee presented its plan for the first and second floors. The sitting room in the southeast corner would be furnished in the period of Iowa Gov. Samuel Kirkwood, meaning the years 1860 to 1875. The room would contain a game table, sofa, velvet-covered chairs, occasional tables, melodeon, and various art objects. The dining room in the southwest corner would feature tables and chairs, sideboards, a display of china, wall hangings, and appropriate fireplace appointments. The library would be furnished in an Oriental motif sometimes found in nineteenth century homes. The music room, which was being restored, would contain as much of B.F. Allen's furniture as could be acquired. Included in the plans were a square rosewood piano, a harp, a sofa, a tete-a-tete, and art objects. The drawing room would be furnished in the style of master Victorian craftsman John Henry Belter, with a sofa, chairs, table, etagere, Oriental rug, mirror, tapestry, and statuary. The receiving room in the mansion's northeast corner would be done in the style of King Louis XV, a style popular in the middle decades of the nineteenth century. The hallway would feature the Gothic style, popular in American-designed furniture from about 1840 to the end of the Civil War. It would include massive thronelike chairs, a hall tree, a Federal table, and hunting trophies. Details concerning second floor furnishings had not been worked out. The Planning Commission recommendations did not carry much weight, though, despite the study that had gone into them. In fact, by the end of 1974, the entire commission was defunct. Even its chairman, Richard Graeme (a Council Bluffs banker who had replaced George Mills), supported the phaseout. Graeme suggested that commission members interested in the future of Terrace Hill join the board of the Terrace Hill Society by pledging $25. As 1974 ended, State Treasurer Baringer announced that the $340,000 on hand was not enough to pay the bills.

It was not until May 1975 that the Executive Council was financially able to award a contract for extensive restoration. But again, bad luck was to strike the project already behind schedule and teetering on insolvency: Antiques donated or lent for use in the mansion were damaged in a warehouse fire. Baringer calculated it would cost between $7,000 and $10,000 to restore the damaged items, which included a set of eight chairs, three large tables, and a Victorian sofa. In addition, it would cost $4,800 to replace a Belter sofa that had been destroyed.

A month after the warehouse fire, the Executive Council halted all renovation work. There was not a cent to pay the bills. The state was short $51,000 on a $93,000 bill submitted by Bergstrom Construction Co. The stoppage did not last long. In two weeks the project resumed because of an unusual step taken by Baringer. He formed an entity called the Terrace Hill Foundation to raise money. The long-range goal was $1.5 million. The foundation was immediately able to obtain a $250,000 loan from Iowa-Des Moines National Bank, the state's largest. The loan allowed renovation to resume. But it also raised questions of impropriety. It struck some observers as wrong that Baringer headed a private corporation requesting loans from institutions with which the state of Iowa might do substantial business. Baringer said later that forming the foundation was not an easy decision. ''The project was out of funds, and I spent a lot of long, sleepless nights wondering how to ethically raise money to keep things going,'' he said.

Even those who did not question where the funding came from were upset about what was being done with it. The Iowa State Historical Board in December 1975 voted to express its concern over the remodeling. Board member Charlene Conklin, chairman of the Terrace Hill Society and a former state senator, said, ''I am terribly worried about what is happening,'' referring to work on the second and third floors. Jack Musgrove, director of the State Historical Museum, also fretted. ''What we need is a group that is willing to stand up and say no to some very important people,'' he said. But none of the critics pushed his views persistently. So Governor Ray and his wife Billie seemed assured of a new home on the top floor, something they felt had been put off too long as it was. The first and second floors were more or less ignored. Supporters of the project wondered why Governor Ray did not use his popularity and influence

Belter sofa destroyed in warehouse fire, September 1975.

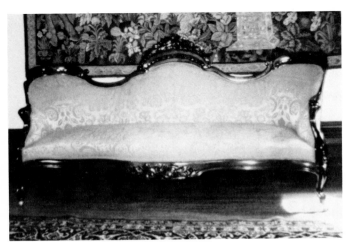

Belter sofa replacement, donated by Daughters of the American Revolution.

to bring in money. What they did not know was that the governor was working to raise money, in his own quiet way. "My opinion was that this was something we did not want to twist arms for," the governor told the authors. "We have talked to people individually, taken them through the house, explained the project to them, then followed it up with a call." Billie Ray said her husband deserved credit, that she would blow his horn if he would not blow his own. "Bob has been a lot more involved than people realize," she said. "Some of the big givers were approached first by Bob or by someone who Bob had asked to raise money. Without Bob, this project would have been dead. Terrace Hill would not even be off the ground, and he has gotten no credit for this that I know of." Whatever the governor was or was not doing, the Terrace Hill Foundation was falling short of its $1.5 million goal. By June 1976, the foundation had borrowed at least $600,000 from banks. Pledges came to $500,000, but some had not been fulfilled. State Sen. William Palmer was angry about the bleak financial picture,

and the resultant delay in opening the house. "We have been fooling with this project for too long," Palmer said. "I don't know how many target dates supporters of Terrace Hill have had for the governor to move in and for the public to use it."

Most members of the public, though, were not overly concerned about the financial problems. Sentiment seemed to be in favor of moving the project along, and hang the cost. It was no wonder many people were impatient to tour Terrace Hill, especially in light of the praise it kept receiving. A survey of Des Moines' "significant architecture" by the city Plan and Zoning Commission said, "The finest Victorian house in Des Moines is Terrace Hill. An example of the Second Empire style, it shows the high mansard roof and multiple dormers characteristic of the tall, bold, three-dimensional style . . ." A separate survey of Iowa architecture, by photographer William Plymat, Jr., said, "Terrace Hill was one of the first and certainly the finest example of American Mansard in Iowa, a style that is also known as Second Empire and General Grant."

Governor Robert Ray, Lu Ann, Billie Ray, Vicki and, seated, Randi Ray, next to west entrance of Terrace Hill, July 1978.

Chapter Fifteen

The Governor's Mansion

As 1976 passed the halfway mark, it appeared that the governor and his family—wife Billie and daughters Randi, LuAnn, and Vicki—would finally leave the former Witmer house to reside in the more private, prestigious Terrace Hill. The Executive Council put the house at 2900 Grand Avenue up for sale, after receiving an appraisal of about $135,000. In early 1977 the Iowa Girls High School Athletic Union was given title in return for $140,000. Governor Ray was pleased to be getting a new official residence, no matter how controversial. Although a down-to-earth man, he had become accustomed to a certain amount of prestige, only natural for someone who had been governor longer than anyone in Iowa history. Born in Des Moines in 1928, Ray graduated from Drake University with degrees in business administration and law. Also attending Drake was Billie Lee Hornberger, who had lived in Des Moines since infancy after being born in Columbus Junction, Iowa. She had attended high school with Ray. While Ray was in law school, Billie taught elementary school in Des Moines. The couple was married in 1951. After a few years practicing law, Ray launched his political career in 1956 by losing a race for Polk County Attorney. In 1958, he was defeated in a bid for the Iowa House of Representatives. But he was never hampered by a loser's image. In 1963, he became chairman of the Iowa Republican Party, building himself a base for a statewide bid. In 1968, he won the Republican gubernatorial nomination at the age of forty, and then defeated Democratic candidate Paul Franzenburg. He was reelected in 1970, 1972, and 1974, when the term of governor was lengthened to four years. The governor scoffed at charges that he would be living ''royally'' in Terrace Hill. ''It's mainly an apartment,'' he told the authors in a 1978 interview. ''The expenses and the charges of royal living miss the mark. We live in a third-floor apartment, period, though it's a nice apartment.''

Moving day was set for October 17, 1976. Iowans were invited to participate in an old-fashioned shivaree, complete with band music and refreshments. The day before the move, members of the Hubbell family were given a private tour of the mansion. One member, Bill Windsor of Des Moines, described what he saw. He noted that a new entranceway and a small porch had been built where a pantry had been on the house's west side. The elevator inside the governor's private entrance was for the exclusive use of the first family. The music room was being restored. The first and second-floor walls were being painted off-white, carpeting was being relaid on the grand staircase, and carpentry was going on all over the mansion. The private staircase from the second to the third floor was finished. The newel-post and a short balustrade were from Cherry Place, a Des Moines mansion at 1204 East Grand Avenue demolished in 1970. Windsor rode the elevator to the Rays' quarters on the third floor, entering the main living room in the northeast corner. To the northwest were the dining room and kitchen, which had powder and laundry rooms adjacent to it. The master bedroom and baths were in the southeast portion. The southwest portion had two additional bedrooms and two baths. The color scheme was mostly greens and yellows. The governor's bath had wallpaper with small elephants (the Republican Party symbol) on it. The tower room would someday, perhaps, be a trophy and barroom.

Moving day went well. But the Rays' move into Terrace Hill was not the end of controversy over the mansion. Within a month, high heating bills at the house were being criticized. The monthly bills approached $2,000. Some of the criticism was valid—the mansion was not energy efficient. But much criticism stemmed from the failure of people to realize that Terrace Hill was not just another house multiplied by two or three. Lawrence Ericsson, one of the architects in charge of renovation, said the utility bills were no surprise because Terrace Hill with its 165,081 cubic feet of heated space was about fourteen times as large as the average residence of 12,000 cubic feet. But, said Ericsson, there was more at work than just the size differential. Terrace Hill needed energy for three side-by-side refrigerator-freezers, an upright freezer, two clothes washers and two dryers, two self-cleaning ovens, a cable television system, two electric steam boilers, an eighty-gallon water heater, and an elevator. Also, Ericsson noted, the house had more than the normal frequency of inside-outside traffic, resulting in a heat loss.

As the cold winter of 1976 turned into the spring of 1977, criticism intensified as the cost of the mansion kept escalating. Legislators insisted the mansion open for public tours by summer. Security guards reported they had to turn away people every day who wanted to see the inside of Terrace Hill. Some of the visitors tried to lie their way inside. The legislature passed a bill requiring that Terrace Hill be opened to the public a minimum of twenty hours a week beginning July 1, 1977, no matter what shape it was in. Ray signed the bill, but objected strongly. He asked the legislature to reconsider. Ray said the east porch, for instance, was in such disrepair that it would have to be off limits to tours, or else visitors might fall through. Ray argued that if citizens saw Terrace Hill in its rundown state, they would have a bad impression of the entire project. The problems of opening the mansion to the public were indeed numerous. The main entrance was in terrible condition, leaving the governor's private entrance on the west side as the only

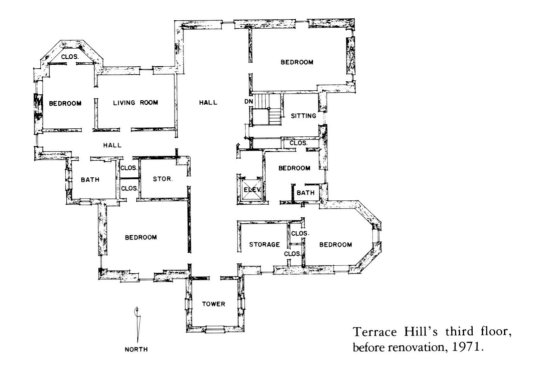

Terrace Hill's third floor,
before renovation, 1971.

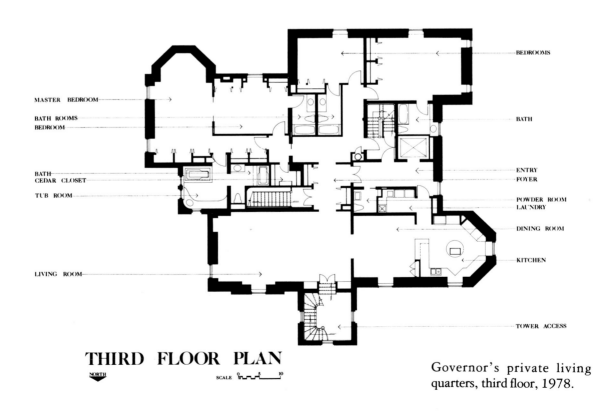

THIRD FLOOR PLAN

NORTH

SCALE 0 5 10

Governor's private living
quarters, third floor, 1978.

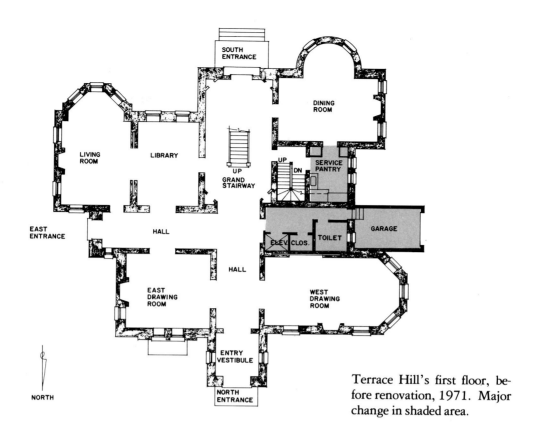

Terrace Hill's first floor, before renovation, 1971. Major change in shaded area.

serviceable one. The driveway was steep, narrow, and unpaved, with almost no room for parking. There were no sidewalks, only bare ground that turned to mud after a rainstorm. There were no public restrooms. The music room restoration had barely begun. The room was stripped to its bare wall studs. Hardware from the sliding wooden doors between the music and drawing rooms had been removed and cataloged by state employees. When it was supposed to be returned, it could not be found. It was thus necessary to recast the pull plates and escutcheons in silver, using the mold of the hardware from the library-sitting room doors. The expense was about $4,000. The second floor was unrestored, with ceilings marred by water stains from a roof that had leaked before being repaired. Furniture awaiting restoration jammed rooms.

State Sen. Earl Willits, a leader in pushing for public access by July 1, 1977, said he realized the validity of Ray's objections. But, Willits said, an obligation had been made by the state in 1971 to open the mansion for public viewing. "That was the agreement when we took it, and that's the way it should be," he said. "It would be years if we waited. I think it's right to force the issue." In response to the governor's objections, Willits said he had asked for estimates of how much it would cost to pave and widen the driveway, rebuild the east porch, and install restrooms. Willits said he would try to convince the legislature to appropriate funds for those improvements, so that some of the mansion could be open by the target date.

Money from the legislature would have been welcome. State Treasurer Baringer said that with $750,000, the project could be finished in six months. Baringer said $1,350,000 had already been spent. The private fund raising was not going well. The Terrace Hill Society, which was concentrating on individual donors, had raised money from medallion sales, memberships, and other sources, but it had already been turned over to the state.

Some expenditures were so pressing that the state went ahead, even though it had to use funds not specifically allocated for Terrace Hill. The Executive Council awarded a $72,000 contract for air conditioning the third floor. Two days before the June 6 vote, the Des Moines temperature was 101 degrees. The Ray family said it had propped open windows with soda pop bottles in an attempt to get the air circulating. "I learned it is hard to sleep when it is that hot," Ray said. "We used all the pop bottles. It is the first time I have ever lived in a third-story attic." The Executive Council decided that the air conditioning would be paid for from the $90,000 left from the sale of the former governor's mansion. The decision was made even though the Iowa-Des Moines National Bank was pressing for that revenue as repayment on its loan for restoration work. The governor did not fight the decision, but even he was ambivalent. "As much as the place needs air conditioning, I would rather get the loan paid off," he said.

A bigger expenditure that raised eyebrows was $104,000 for a security system. Here is how a newspaper account described it: "Around the perimeter of the towering Victorian mansion, there will run a sophisticated black-light cable. The unsuspecting intruder instantly will alert guards when crossing it. Television cameras will constantly survey the grounds, relaying to a control panel evidence of anything suspicious. Doors will be secured with expensive locks, and roads leading to the mansion will be blocked by electronic gates costing thousands of dollars. Approaching visitors will be questioned

Governor's private west entrance, attached to former butler's pantry. (Courtesy Lawrence Ericsson.)

Governor's third floor living quarters.

Third floor dining room; chandelier from 2900 Grand.

Northwest kitchen area, third floor.

Laundry facility adjacent to kitchen and elevator.

through an intercom system. Guards with the best available hand-held two-way radios will patrol the grounds. A generator will stand by to provide lighting should an emergency strike. And if, by a stroke of luck, an intruder makes it through the black light, past the gates and locks and television cameras and radios to the very walls of the mansion, his footsteps will surely be detected on the pressure-sensitive sensor mats that will be hidden underfoot.'' State trooper Earl Usher, in charge of the governor's safety, acknowledged that the devices were more elaborate than what had existed in the former mansion. Usher said the new system was needed because ''there is going to be a lot of valuable stuff on the bottom floors of the mansion. If it was just the governor and his family living there, you maybe would not need as much. But when you open it up to the public, you need to know what is going on.'' The $104,000 price tag did not include about $50,000 in annual salaries for the guards.

During 1977 it seemed that talk of Terrace Hill's financial squeeze was continual. The legislature and governor worked out a compromise over funding and public access. The House and the Senate agreed to postpone mandatory public tours until July 1, 1978, and to give the Executive Council $125,000 to do what was needed so public access would be practical. The bill said the $125,000 would have to be matched from private sources.

Shortly after the legislative action, Governor Ray named a new group to direct the Terrace Hill project. The action superseded the groups that had been operating—formally and informally—to move the project forward: The disbanded Terrace Hill Planning Commission, the Terrace Hill Society, and the Terrace Hill Foundation. Ray chose the members of the new Terrace Hill Authority carefully. He could say without fear of contradiction that the members provided a good mix of business management and historic preservation knowledge. But, skeptics noted, there was something the governor did not say—that by appointing the eight members, he was attempting to consolidate his power over the way the mansion would turn out. And, those skeptics noted, the governor left nothing to chance: He specifically designated Billie Ray to be his representative at Authority meetings. She was sure to carry weight in any deliberations, partly because she was an impressive figure in her own right, partly because she was the governor's wife, and partly because she did, after all, have to live with whatever was done to the house.

The other members of the Terrace Hill Authority were Adrian Anderson, director of the Historic Preservation Division of the State Historical Department in Iowa City; State Treasurer Maurice Baringer; Robert Bates of Albia, an interior designer and the only member representing the Terrace Hill Society; John Fitzgibbon, president of the Iowa-Des Moines National Bank; Margaret Keyes, a University of Iowa professor who had overseen the restoration of Old Capitol in Iowa City; Robert Schoeller, a Des Moines interior designer who assisted with the Rays' third-floor quarters; and Authority Chairman Richard Thomas of Mount Vernon, a professor of history at Cornell College.

The Terrace Hill Authority immediately found itself embroiled in squabbles. An October 18, 1977, review of the mansion's funding in the *Des Moines Tribune* summarized the problems: ''Back in 1972, when it was suggested that the legislature make Terrace Hill into a combination governor's residence and historical site, nobody knew how much it would cost. A figure of $250,000 was tossed around, and there was talk of the project taking two years. Later, the estimate was raised to $550,000, and Terrace Hill boosters were affronted when critics said it might run more than $1 million. Now, five years later, more than $1.5 million has been spent and the project is still years away from completion. The project is more than $700,000 in debt, and nobody connected with the project is estimating ultimate costs.'' State Senator Willits predicted the price tag would top $3 million, noting, ''We could have built a beautiful new mansion for $1 million. At the time I supported it, but in retrospect it was a mistake. We never got any accurate cost figures. Terrace Hill's boosters just weren't being realistic.'' Rural Iowans, too, joined the criticism. Architect Wagner was the object of attacks in the northwest Iowa weekly *Holstein Advance,* which termed him the man ''who has made so many obvious blunders on the governor's mansion.''

Despite such carping, Authority Chairman Thomas was confident the group would bring the project under control by offering it unified direction. The gloomy balance sheet did not depress Thomas, who noted, ''There are people in the state who have indicated a willingness to donate substantially, provided there was some sense of direction and real expertise. I think the prospects for that magnificent property are quite good. I hope we can convey a sense of confidence. We are fixing a building we hope will last for another one hundred years or more. Documentation indicates there was simply no other structure like Terrace Hill anywhere in the Midwest at the time it was built.''

Baringer, a member of the Authority who had been a key member of its various predecessor groups, said many of the serious problems were in the past. ''The major problem was that the building is 110 years old,'' he said. ''There was more concealed deterioration than we anticipated.'' For example, a new sewer system was needed because raw sewage was being drained into the ground under the house. The wiring had become so frayed that it seemed miraculous the mansion had not burned decades earlier. New plumbing, a new boiler, and outside water lines were necessary, and the roof needed not only waterproofing but also structural reinforcement. There was ignorance over how much some types of restoration would cost. The original stenciled ceiling and wall decorations had been painted over in the 1920s. Purists wanted the stenciling restored—until they found out the cost for that alone would

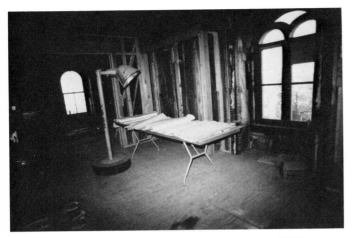

Master bedroom suite under construction, 1975.

Carpet for master bedroom suite, 1976.

Before renovation; gutted servants' bathroom, 1976. Trapdoor in ceiling joists previously led to smaller tower on the roof.

Renovated master bath features a sunken tub and view of the entire downtown Des Moines.

Governor's master bath suite features a sunken tub, shower, and wall treatments in an elephant motif and golden marbled foil.

approach $500,000. And then there was the nemesis of all building projects: inflation. Baringer said construction costs were rising 10 percent a month during certain periods. He said if the legislature had appropriated enough money in 1973 to get the work done quickly, much of the inflation would have been avoided; costs probably would have been cut in half.

The costs of Terrace Hill were provided by Baringer to the Authority as that body started to act with vigor in mid-September 1977. The balance sheet breakdown looked like this: expenditures to stabilize the mansion and meet building codes, $520,948; expenditures for third-floor occupancy, $413,088; general repairs, insulation, air conditioning, painting, $499,314; architectural and engineering fees and studies, $174,756. When other items were added, total expenditures came to $1,628,106.

The income side of the balance sheet was as large, but nearly half of the income was in the form of loans to the Terrace Hill Foundation. Those loans had to be repaid.

Although repayment of the long-term financing was nettlesome, the Authority's immediate worry was finding money to allow public tours starting July 1, 1978. The pressure was eased when the state received $391,000 from the U.S. Economic Development Administration to go with the conditional $125,000 from the Iowa General Assembly. At its October 1977 meeting, the Authority heard a report from member Adrian Anderson. Anderson's theme was that there could be no successful public tours by the summer deadline unless a system were established to manage the Terrace Hill site. The first step would be to find a site manager and hire tour guides.

At the same meeting, the Terrace Hill Authority adopted a statement outlining how the house would be restored from thereon. It read: ''The long history of the home and the changes that have occurred over this occupancy make it impossible to establish the exact decor and furnishings of rooms. Rather than restore the first-floor rooms and selected second-floor rooms to a specific family (Allen or Hubbell), the Authority established the post-Civil War period to 1900 as the era which will determine the restoration, decoration, and furnishing. Thus the aim is to illustrate the mood and character of the period as it was lived by the Iowa gentry. The basic guide for first-floor development will be the photographic evidence at hand of the home in the established period. This means an attempt to restore and furnish to the early Hubbell period. However, it does not mean to restore every detail of the rooms as documented by the photos. The commitment is to the period, and not the family. Careful documentation of gentry homes of this period is available and will be used in selecting the architectural interior environment of the house. The Authority recognizes the uniqueness of the Allens' and Hubbells' special place among the gentry of the state and seeks to present as much of the elegance of these families as possible.''

All that was easier said than done, especially because the Authority entered the picture so late. At its November 1977 meeting, Billie Ray complained that a new basement restroom was not in keeping with the way things had been in the time of the Allens and Hubbells. Describing the tiled floor and the stainless steel fixtures, Mrs. Ray said the men's facility looked ''about like a Standard Oil station restroom.'' The Authority designated member Robert Schoeller, an interior designer, to examine the restroom and report back. Schoeller looked at it the next day, and commented, with some understatement: ''It kind of breaks the spell of the rest of the house.'' At its December 1977 meeting, the Authority, with regrets, told Mrs. Ray that the men's restroom would have to stay the way it was. The group decided, however, that a women's restroom still to be constructed would be as Victorian in appearance as possible.

The Authority had bigger problems to solve as 1977 drew to a close. The $391,000 grant from the federal government was in jeopardy because of a federal law saying 10 percent of the money had to go to a contractor who was a minority group member. In all Iowa, there were not more than twenty such contractors. Baringer expressed concern: ''I am worried because we do not have all that many minority businesses involved in remodeling-type construction. We are scrounging.'' Another problem the Authority had to wrestle with was a recommendation by the architects that no further construction begin until a large amount of money was available. Because so much work had been done piecemeal, the architects were finding themselves in the embarrassing position of ordering some previous work torn out. New plumbing had to be routed around existing steam pipes when it was discovered that the third floor needed more heat. Later, when heat ducts and registers were installed, the new steam pipes had to be rerouted. Yet another problem was the resistance in the legislature to providing the money needed to run Terrace Hill, not including any of the renovation. The estimate was about $330,000 annually, more than half of it for security.

Knowing that legislative appropriations would never be enough, Terrace Hill's backers, pushed by Governor Ray, heightened efforts to raise money from the private sector. The Terrace Hill Foundation recruited top businessmen to raise money from the commercial community. One of the top fundraisers was Robb Kelley, president of Employers Mutual Insurance Companies in Des Moines. Kelley reported that a fund drive which began November 1, 1977, had led to business pledges topping $400,000 over a three-year period. The Terrace Hill Society concentrated on individuals, working through Democratic and Republican leaders in each of Iowa's ninety-nine counties. There were also about 26,000 Terrace Hill medallions remaining to be sold of the original 94,000 minted in 1972. The price had jumped from $15 to $20 for the silver medallions, and from $2.50 to $10 for the bronze medallions. About 3,400 of the bronze medallions had become tarnished in storage.

East drive approaching Terrace Hill.

West side driveway.

Antique photographs of Terrace Hill taken in the late nineteenth century. (Courtesy William Wagner.)

The travails of Terrace Hill could not knock the positive profiles out of the news, though. American Federal Savings and Loan Association in Des Moines featured the mansion in a magazine distributed to its customers. There was nothing but praise for the project: ''Terrace Hill is a credit to the people and state of Iowa. The historical value of the mansion is impossible to measure. But certainly future generations of Iowans will be grateful to the people of Iowa, the Hubbell family, the Terrace Hill Society, and the Terrace Hill Foundation for their efforts in preservation and restoration.'' The *Des Moines Register* ran a color picture spread of the third floor. Although the third floor distressed some knowledgeable observers because it was in no way consistent with a 110-year-old Victorian mansion, the newspaper's account did not even hint at discord. The third floor was termed ''attractive and comfortable.'' The article described how the height of the ceilings had made it possible to raise the floor more than two feet so that the plumbing and wiring could be laid beneath it. Walls were ripped out, making the living space more ''airy.'' The colors throughout the third floor were bright yellow, grass green, gold, copper, and nasturtium. Soft maize-colored carpeting was laid, except in the kitchen, some of the baths and hallways; the hallway floors were polished wood parquet. The furnishings were a mixture of state-owned items and those privately owned by the Rays. In the living room, where a cherry mantelpiece had been installed, two velvet gold chairs were placed along with a sofa and a wing chair covered in prints repeating the color of the curtains. The dining room was furnished largely with items from the former governor's mansion. Many of those items were slated for removal to the formal first-floor dining room when it was restored. Mrs. Ray was pleased with the third floor. ''The place did look very unhomelike at first,'' she said, ''but all that wonderful space was there and it was not hard to imagine what could be done with it.''

One positive report concerning Terrace Hill seemed to capture the imagination of many Iowans. Robert Harvey, an Iowa State University professor of landscape architecture, discovered through research how the Terrace Hill grounds had looked in the days of B.F. Allen. There had been some evidence in old photographs, but Harvey went beyond that information. The grounds had featured exotic plantings, flower banks, vineyards, orchards, and walks. Harvey was hoping to restore the original landscaping, although he knew limited funds made it a far-off project. Besides, he wanted to develop a master plan; he was in no hurry.

Soon after Harvey's ideas were published, the Terrace Hill project received another boost when Miss Lillian Carter, the popular, colorful mother of the President of the United States, stayed overnight in Des Moines. She slept at Terrace Hill, a Democrat in the home of the Republican first family. During Miss Lillian's visit, Billie Ray commented that Terrace Hill had been undergoing renovation for ''a long, long time.'' The comment sounded wistful. But if Mrs. Ray were silently

East porches. Note the change in the shape of the porch compared with the present.

Former greenhouse and flowerbeds behind Terrace Hill.

hoping that the end was in sight, her hope was dashed by a report to the Terrace Hill Authority from architect Ericsson. The report, dated December 13, 1977, said decisions had to be made quickly for federally funded work to proceed on schedule. Some decisions involved the basement rooms, especially the parts that would be seen by the public. "If a Victorian-esque period decor is desired, we could certainly comply," Ericsson said. "However, our recommendation is that a more functional and much less costly direction be taken . . . . There are insufficient funds to permit ornate Victorian wood door casings, wood baseboards, marble countertops, etcetera." On the second floor, Ericsson recommended that some areas remain uncompleted, at least until there was enough money to do everything under one contract. Ericsson anticipated Mrs. Ray's dismay at the report, but said everything possible was being done to ease the burden on the first family: "We have in the past specified that the contractors must make every effort to coordinate their activities with the functions of the governor's family, and that they respect the privacy of the family. But there will no doubt be times when functions will clash and disruption of the household staff will be inevitable."

Ericsson's statement was a vivid portrayal of all the things—big and little, expected and unexpected—that could go wrong during a renovation project on the scale of Terrace Hill's. Some of the problems had unquestionably arisen from poor planning, second-rate management, and naivete. The magnitude of the cost overruns at times made the Pentagon look frugal. But, as already noted, most Iowans had not lost faith in the project, even through the worst of times. An editorial in the *Des Moines Register* of December 27, 1977, probably summarized the prevailing mood. The editorial was headlined "Terrace Hill Drags On." It said: "The high hopes that surrounded the state's acquisition of Terrace Hill more than six years ago have diminished as the more mundane chores of restoring the old Victorian mansion have demanded increasing attention. The project is an easy target for uninformed criticism ('a white elephant') and partisan sniping ('a palace for Governor Ray'). It is appropriate, in view of the flagging enthusiasm, for private and public backers of the restoration project to join in a concerted effort to finish the job as quickly as possible. . . . Roughly one million dollars is needed to wrap up the restoration project. That would put total costs in the neighborhood of $2.5 million. It sounds like a lot, but it is not outlandish considering the magnitude of the project and the special care required to duplicate many nineteenth century structural features. . . . Many Iowans have become impatient with the slow pace of the Terrace Hill project. We urge the project leaders, both in and out of government, to join in an effort to speed up the work."

Calls for an end to bickering were not enough, however. Partisanship in the legislature bedeviled Terrace Hill in early 1978. State Rep. Richard Byerly, a Democrat, suggested that Iowa's governors be provided with $600 a month for rent and utilities, and that in return the state stop providing a mansion for governors. Byerly said taxpayers were providing the Ray family with a life of "regal splendor" in Terrace Hill. Byerly's proposal lost after much discussion. One surprise opponent was State Sen. Willits, a frequent critic of the project. Willits had his reasons: "We have Terrace Hill. It's been a fiasco, but we've got it and at this point we've spent so much money that we might as well finish it and make someone accountable for it." Soon after Byerly's proposal, Tom Whitney, a Democratic candidate for governor, got in his licks by announcing that if he defeated Robert Ray, he would not reside in Terrace Hill. Whitney, a member of the Polk County Board of Supervisors, resurrected the high energy bill controversy in his

announcement. "The governor's home costs $27,000 a year to heat and cool," Whitney said. "That's the kind of energy example the governor of Iowa sets."

Legislators, especially the Democrats, took up the cry of energy waste, too. Rep. Norman Jesse said the energy bills were so horrendous that "we ought to have the attorney general sue the architect for malpractice." Jesse, one of the legislature's most eloquent debaters, was angry about the entire budget submitted for the operation of Terrace Hill. The amount requested was $296,300, several times what Jesse said was the $80,000 budget for the former mansion at 2900 Grand Avenue. There were more people operating Terrace Hill. At 2900 Grand, Governor Ray had one security guard, three Iowa High-

Southeast lawn.

Southwest lawn near Terrace Hill.

South entrance.

Carriage house, east side. Note the lattice-enclosed addition on the far left side of photo, no longer there today.

Governor and Mrs. Robert D. Ray greet Iowa citizens on July 2, 1978, at the first official open house.

Tom McKay, temporary site coordinator; Richard Thomas, Billie and Governor Ray at open house July 2, 1978.

way Patrol bodyguards, one cook, one maintenance worker, and one custodian. At Terrace Hill, according to the budget request, there was a need for six security guards, three state patrol officers, one cook, three maintenance workers, two custodians, a gardener, two tour guides, and a site coordinator. Despite the partisan potshots, the House approved the $296,300 figure. Earlier, the Senate had voted the same sum. But House members would not agree to an amendment by Republican Rep. Laverne Schroeder to provide $600,000 to help complete restoration. Most legislators believed the work had already cost too much.

The Rays tried to keep themselves above the controversy by pushing for broad public support for the project. Billie Ray said she was oblivious to the criticism: ''We get letters from all over the country about Terrace Hill. People from out of state drive by to look. It will be a living museum, and I appreciate what people have done for it.'' Privately, persons close to the project complained about shoddy workmanship. The emphasis, these informed critics said off-the-record, was on doing whatever had to be done to open the mansion for tours by July 1978. The second floor was being ignored, since the decision had been made that it would be off-limits to the public. And faithful restoration of the six first-floor rooms had been thrown to the winds. Visitors would not be seeing the rooms as they looked in the days of the Allens and the Hubbells.

Yet when the mansion was opened for viewing July 2, the 850 visitors from all over Iowa and at least a dozen other states were not griping. A newspaper reporter who interviewed many of the people walking through noted that ''for all the controversy that has surrounded the home since it was donated to the state, none was heard from Sunday's visitors.'' A Cedar Rapids woman seemed to speak for the group when she said, ''It's a beautiful place. Just absolutely beautiful. I think it's money well spent.'' The woman's daughter chimed in, ''I can't imagine anyone living here—it's just too grand.'' Terrace Hill had survived another round of controversy. Its legend lived on.

East porch removed and reconstructed, March 1978.

Entrance canopy undergoes restoration, March 1978.

South entrance reconstruction, early 1978.

Music room adjoining drawing room, July 2, 1978.

Library, July 2, 1978.

Dining room and bay, dining room and breakfront, July 2, 1978.

Scherrie Goettsch, a native of Holstein, Iowa, has a longtime interest in old houses and furniture. She became fascinated with Terrace Hill while attending Drake University in Des Moines, where she earned a degree in interior design. She lived at Terrace Hill as a caretaker in 1971-72. Since then, she has worked at the Iowa State Historical Museum and taught art in the Des Moines public schools.

Steve Weinberg, her husband, has worked as a reporter on the *Des Moines Register* and taught journalism at Drake University and the University of Missouri. He has published articles in numerous magazines. He has an intense interest in local history.

Photo by Warren Taylor

Ink drawing by Amy N. Worthen.

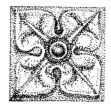

Illustrations

Ink drawings at chapter headings and endings are of designs found throughout Terrace Hill. Chapter one is taken from the parquetry in the vestibule and main hall. Chapter two is the wood carving on the vestibule hall tree. Chapter three is from the reception room fireplace facing. The same room provided a parquetry design for Chapter four. Chapters five through ten show more compositions from the facing around the drawing room fireplace mantel. Chapter eleven too, is a detail of the facing around the dining room fireplace. Chapters twelve through fourteen show wood carvings on the built-in breakfront in the dining room. In Chapter fifteen a portion of the white marble mantel in the sitting room can be found.

Chapter one ends with a detail of the sitting room fireplace mantel. Stencil designs as seen on the walls in Terrace Hill in the 1890s provide endings for Chapters two, three, five and fourteen. Chapter two is taken from the ceiling border in the main hall. Chapter three's egg and dart (life and death) stencil is in the dissecting east-west hall above the dado. Chapter five shows a ceiling border taken from the present day library, originally the billiard room. Chapter fourteen is an extension of the ceiling border design found in the main hall surrounding the grand stair. Detail shown here is from the first floor back stair's newel post. Table of Contents page shows a design taken from the dinning room breakfront. The finale is a detail of the lion's head on the mausoleum door of F.M. Hubbell. (Ink designs by Scherrie Goettsch.)

Photographs

All photographs taken by Scherrie Goettsch, unless noted otherwise.

Bibliography

Books

Allen, William G. *A History of Story County, Iowa.* Des Moines: Iowa Printing Co., 1887.

Andreas, Alfred T. *Historical Atlas of the State of Iowa.* Chicago: Andreas Atlas Co., 1875.

Andrews, Lorenzo F. *Pioneers of Polk County, Iowa, and Reminiscences of Early Days.* 2 vols. Des Moines: Baker-Trisler Co., 1908.

Bentley, Nicolas. *The Victorian Scene: 1837-1901.* London: George Weidenfeld and Nicolson, 1968.

Brigham, Johnson. *Des Moines, the Pioneer of Municipal Progress and Reform of the Middle West.* 3 vols. Chicago: S.J. Clarke Publishing Co., 1911.

————. *Iowa: Its History and Foremost Citizens.* Chicago: S.J. Clarke Publishing Co., 1916.

Brown, Leonard. *Poems of the Prairies.* Des Moines: Redhead and Wellslager, 1868.

Bushnell, Joseph P. *City Directory of Des Moines.* Des Moines: Joseph P. Bushnell, 1871. (Various other Des Moines city and business directories were consulted, some compiled by Bushnell, others by different editors.)

Cole, Cyrenus. *I Remember, I Remember.* Iowa City: State Historical Society of Iowa, 1936.

Condit, Carl W. *The Chicago School of Architecture.* Chicago: University of Chicago Press, 1964.

Conran, Terence. *The Kitchen Book.* New York: Crown Publishers Inc., 1977.

Des Moines Plan and Zoning Commission. *Des Moines' Heritage: A Survey of Significant Architecture.* Des Moines, 1976.

Dixon, J.M., ed. *Centennial History of Polk County, Iowa.* Des Moines: State Register Printers, 1876.

Erickson, Erling A. *Banking in Frontier Iowa, 1836 to 1865.* Ames, Iowa: Iowa State University Press, 1971.

Greater Des Moines Chamber of Commerce Federation. *The Spirit of Seventy Six: A History of the Greater Des Moines Chamber of Commerce Federation.* Des Moines, 1976.

Greiff, Constance M., ed. *Lost America—Part I: From the Atlantic to the Mississippi River.* Princeton, N.J.: Pyne Press, 1971.

Grodinsky, Julius. *The Iowa Pool: A Study in Railroad Competition, 1870-74.* Chicago: University of Chicago Press, 1954.

Harlan, Edgar Rubey. *A Narrative History of the People of Iowa.* 5 vols. Chicago: American Historical Society Inc., 1931.

Harris, Cyril M., ed. *Historic Architecture Sourcebook.* New York: McGraw-Hill Book Co., 1977.

Hirshson, Stanley P. *Grenville M. Dodge: Soldier, Politician, Railroad Pioneer.* Bloomington, Ind.: Indiana University Press, 1967.

Hubbell, Walter. *History of the Hubbell Family, Containing a Genealogical Record.* New York: J.H. Hubbell and Co., 1881.

Hussey, Tacitus. *Beginnings: Reminiscences of Early Des Moines.* Des Moines: American Lithography and Printing Co., 1919.

————. *The Biography of Edwin Ruthven Clapp, a Pioneer of Des Moines.* Des Moines: Register and Leader Co., 1906.

Iowa American Revolution Bicentennial Commission. *Iowa and the U.S. Bicentennial.* Des Moines, 1976.

Iowa State Historical Department, Division of Historic Preservation. *Plumb Grove—The Governor Robert Lucas Home.* Iowa City, 1977.

James, F. Cyril. *The Growth of Chicago Banks.* 2 vols. New York: Harper and Brothers, 1938.

Jubilee Year Semi-centennial of the Organization of Polk County and Fort Des Moines, Iowa. Des Moines: Carter and Hussey, 1896.

Kilburn, Lucian M., ed. *History of Adair County, Iowa, and Its People.* Chicago: Pioneer Publishing Co., 1915.

LeVander, Iantha, ed. *Where Your Governors Live.* Privately published, 1969.

Merritt, Fred D. *The Early History of Banking in Iowa.* Iowa City: University Press, 1900.

Mills, George, with Joan Bunke, ed. *Harvey Ingham and Gardner Cowles, Sr.: Things Don't Just Happen.* Ames, Iowa: Iowa State University Press, 1977.

Mills, George S. *The Little Man With the Long Shadow.* Des Moines: Trustees of the Frederick M. Hubbell Estate, 1955.

Nourse, Charles Clinton. *The Autobiography of Charles Clinton Nourse.* Privately published, 1911.

Pease, George Sexton. *Patriarch of the Prairie: The Story of Equitable of Iowa, 1867-1967.* New York: Appleton-Century-Crofts, 1967.

Peglow, Pam, ed. *Iowa Official Register, 1975-1976.* Des Moines: Vern Lundquist, state superintendent of printing, 1975.

Perkins, Jacob R. *Trails, Rails and War: The Life of General G.M. Dodge.* Indianapolis: Bobbs-Merrill Co., 1929.

Pioneer Law-Makers Association of Iowa, Reunion of 1894. Des Moines: G.H. Ragsdale, state printer, 1894.

Plymat, William, Jr. *The Victorian Architecture of Iowa.* Des Moines: Elephant's Eye Inc., 1976.

Porter, Will. *Annals of Polk County and the City of Des Moines.* Des Moines: George A. Miller Printing Co., 1898.

Pratt, LeRoy. *From Cabin to Capital.* Des Moines: State Department of Public Instruction, 1974.

Preston, Howard H., with Benjamin F. Shambaugh, ed. *History of Banking in Iowa.* Iowa City: The State Historical Society of Iowa, 1922.

Randall, Frank A. *History of the Development of Building Construction in Chicago.* Urbana, Ill.: University of Illinois Press, 1949.

Sage, Leland. *A History of Iowa.* Ames, Iowa: Iowa State University Press, 1974.

————. *William Boyd Allison: A Study in Practical Politics.* Iowa City: State Historical Society of Iowa, 1956.

Sanford, N., Mrs. *Early Sketches of Polk County From 1842-1860.* Newton, Iowa: Charles A. Clark, printer, 1874.

Stevens, Warder W. *Centennial History of Washington County, Indiana.* Indianapolis: B.F. Bowen and Co. Inc., 1916.

Stiles, Edward H. *Recollections and Sketches of Notable Lawyers and Public Men of Early Iowa.* Des Moines: Homestead Publishing Co., 1916.

Swierenga, Robert. *Acres for Cents: Delinquent Tax Auctions in Frontier Iowa.* Westport, Conn.: Greenwood Press, 1976.

————. *Pioneers and Profits: Land Speculation on the Iowa Frontier.* Ames, Iowa: The Iowa State University Press, 1968.

Taylor, Henry and Co., ed. *Compendium of History and Biography of Cass County, Iowa.* Chicago: Henry Taylor and Co., 1906.

Throne, Mildred. *Cyrus Clay Carpenter and Iowa Politics, 1854-1898.* Iowa City: State Historical Society of Iowa, 1974.

Turrill, H.B. *Historical Reminiscences of the City of Des Moines.* Des Moines: Redhead and Dawson, 1857.

Williams, Henry Lionel, and Williams, Ottalie K. *Great Houses of America.* New York: G.P. Putnam's Sons, 1966.

Withey, Henry F., and Withey, Elsie Rathburn. *Biographical Dictionary of American Architects (Deceased).* Los Angeles: Hennessey and Ingalls Inc., 1970.

Younger, Edward. *John A. Kasson: Politics and Diplomacy From Lincoln to McKinley.* Iowa City: State Historical Society of Iowa, 1955.

Periodicals

American Dream, a publication of American Federal Savings and Loan Association, Des Moines. Vol. 3 (Spring 1977), "Finally . . . . A Tenant for Terrace Hill."

American Heritage. Vol. 6 (October 1955), John Maas, "In Defense of the Victorian House."

Annals of Iowa. Vol. 2 (January 1896), John M. Brainard, "Opening an Iowa County."

_____. Vol. 4 (January 1900), John A. Kasson, "The Fight for the New Capitol."

_____. Vol. 4 (April 1900), Tacitus Hussey, "History of Steamboating on the Des Moines River From 1837 to 1862."

_____. Vol. 5 (July 1901), Hoyt Sherman, "The State Bank of Iowa."

_____. Vol. 11 (April 1914), Frank M. Mills, "Early Commercial Travelling in Iowa."

_____. Vol. 12 (October 1920), obituary of B.F. Allen.

_____. Vol. 13 (January 1922), Charles Keyes, "Calvin Webb Keyes, Iowa Centenarian."

_____. Vol. 15 (January 1926), George Gallarno, "How Iowa Cared for Orphans of Her Soldiers of the Civil War."

_____. Vol. 16 (October 1928), short item on B.F. Allen.

_____. Vol. 16 (April 1929), David C. Mott, "Pioneer Lawmakers Association."

_____. Vol. 17 (January 1931), obituary of F.M. Hubbell.

_____. Vol. 20 (January 1937), letter from W.R. Sawhill concerning the ancestry of B.F. Allen.

_____. Vol. 33 (April 1957), obituary of Grover Hubbell.

_____. Vol. 41 (Spring 1972), Linda K. Thomson, "Terrace Hill, A Magnificent Gift to the State of Iowa."

_____. Vol. 44 (Summer 1977), Louise Noun, "Annie Savery: a Voice for Women's Rights."

Association for Preservation Technology. Vol. 9, No. 3 (1977), Robert R. Harvey, "Documenting a Victorian Landscape in the Midwest."

DKQ Review, a regional business report of Dain, Kalman and Quail Inc., Minneapolis, Minnesota. Vol. 4 (Spring 1972).

Dividend, a publication of Equitable Life Insurance Co. of Iowa, Des Moines, Vol. 11 (October 1960), "Welcome to Terrace Hill."

_____. Vol. 27 (December 1976), Bill Windsor, "Terrace Hill Revisited."

Equiowa, a publication of Equitable Life Insurance Co. of Iowa, Des Moines. Vol. 64, No. 4 (1977), an interview with James W. Hubbell, Jr.

Inland Architect and Builder. Vol. 6, No. 1 (August 1885).

Iowa Architect. Vol. 21 (October-December 1974), William Wagner, "Terrace Hill."

Iowa Journal of History and Politics. Vol. 11 (January 1913), "Captain James Allen's Dragoon Expedition From Fort Des Moines, Territory of Iowa, in 1884."

_____. Vol. 32, No. 1 (1934), Ruth A. Gallaher, "Money in Pioneer Iowa."

_____. Vol. 39, No. 1 (1941), Jacob A. Swisher, "The Capitols at Des Moines."

_____. Vol. 46 (July 1948), Luella M. Wright, "Leonard Brown, Poet and Populist."

_____. Vol. 48 (October 1950), Mildred Throne, "Electing an Iowa Governor, 1871: Cyrus Clay Carpenter."

Iowan. Vol. 3 (February-March 1955), "Terrace Hill."

Land Owner. Vol. 6 (February 1874), "Prominent Men of the West: Hon. B.F. Allen."

Midwestern. Vol. 1 (February 1907), L.F. Andrews, "The Beginnings of Insurance in Des Moines."

_____. Vol. 2 (April 1908), "Manufacturing Interests in Des Moines."

Palimpsest. Vol. 45 (October 1964), Frank P. Donovan, "The Wabash in Iowa."

_____. Vol. 47 (November 1966), Genevieve P. Mauck, "Grenville Mellon Dodge, Soldier-Engineer."

Picture, the magazine of the Des Moines Sunday Register. December 12, 1971, "Studying Future of Terrace Hill."

_____. July 7, 1974, George Mills, "Terrace Hill, Its Future and Those Medallions."

Postal History Journal. October 1976 and subsequent issues, James S. Leonardo, "The Postal History of Des Moines, Iowa."

Transmission, a publication of Northern Natural Gas Co., Omaha, Nebraska. Vol. 20, No. 4 (1971), "Terrace Hill, a Victorian Jewel."

Newspapers

The following newspapers were searched for material relating to Terrace Hill, Benjamin Franklin Allen, Frederick Marion Hubbell, and other people and places:

Chicago Times, 1875-1887.

Chicago Tribune, 1875-1877.

Des Moines Capital, 1913-1914.

Des Moines Daily News, 1883-1914.

Des Moines Gazette, 1850.

Des Moines Leader, 1895.
Des Moines Plain Talk, 1914.
Des Moines Register, 1897-1978.
Des Moines Register and Leader, 1905-1914.
Des Moines Tribune, 1929-1978.
Hartford (Connecticut) *Daily Courant*, 1877.
Iowa Citizen, 1858.
Iowa Daily State Register, 1867-1884.
Iowa State Journal, 1876-1877.
Iowa State Leader, 1877.
Iowa State Register. 1873-1902.
Marshall (Marshalltown, Iowa) *Times*, 1871.
New York Herald. 1877.
New York Times, 1877-1930.
Rocky Mountain (Denver, Colorado) *News*, 1880.
Salem (Indiana) *Democrat*, 1879.
Sioux City Eagle, 1857.
Sioux City Journal, 1972.

Interviews

Baringer, Maurice. Iowa State Treasurer, February 7, 1978.

Beers, Robert. Hubbell Realty Co., in-person and telephone, various occasions, 1977 and 1978.

Ericsson, Lawrence. Architect on Terrace Hill project, February 6, 1978, and subsequent occasions.

Hubbell, James W., Jr. Trustee of the estate of F.M. Hubbell, February 10, 1978.

Ingham, Frances. Granddaughter of F.M. Hubbell, various occasions, 1977 and 1978.

McCausland, Stanley. Iowa State General Services Department, February 2, 1978.

Ray, Robert, and Ray, Billie. Governor and first lady of Iowa, February 14, 1978.

Synhorst, Melvin. Iowa secretary of state, February 6, 1978.

Wagner, William. Architect on Terrace Hill project, various occasions, 1977 and 1978.

Windsor, Mary Belle. Granddaughter of F.M. Hubbell, various occasions, 1977 and 1978.

Academic Theses

Agnew, Dwight L. "Beginnings of the Rock Island Lines, 1851-1870." Ph.D. dissertation, University of Iowa, 1947.

Busse, Grace Margaret. "A History of the *Des Moines Register.*" Master's thesis, University of Iowa, 1932.

Governmental and Quasi-Governmental Documents

Census of the United States. 1850, 1860, 1870, 1880.

Census of the State of Iowa. 1885, 1895, 1905, 1915, 1925.

Iowa Board of Railroad Commissioners. Annual reports, 1878-1908.

Iowa General Assembly. Report of the special committee appointed by the House of Representatives of the Seventh General Assembly to investigate alleged frauds in the location of the Capitol. 1858.

———. House File 1196, Sixty-fourth General Assembly, first session, 1972.

———. House Journal, March 23, 1972.

———. Senate File 3571, May 12, 1977.

Iowa Geological Survey. Annual report for 1894, Vol. 2, article on Iowa coal deposits.

———. Annual report for 1908, Vol. 19.

Iowa Insurance Department. Historical summary of insurance companies doing business in the state.

Iowa Supreme Court. Allen v. Loring, 37 Iowa 596; 1873.

———. Ringgold County v. Allen, 42 Iowa 697; 1876.

———. In Re Hubbell Trust, 135 Iowa 637; 1907.

———. Frederick M. Hubbell, et al., v. Lafayette Higgins, 148 Iowa 36; 1910.

Polk County District Court. Test cases filed by the Hubbell trust. Nos. CE 1 281, October 12, 1973; CE 3 1237, October 9, 1974; CE 4 2303, November 7, 1975; CE 6 3228, October 7, 1976; CE 8 4208, October 20, 1977.

Polk County Recorder's Office. Mortgage deed, Frances E. Hubbell and husband to B.F. Allen, May 9, 1884.

———. Deed, Hoyt Sherman to Polk and Hubbell, 1884, Book 115, Page 604.

———. Instrument creating the Hubbell trust, 1904, Book 455, Page 555, and Book 473, Page 58.

State of Iowa. Terrace Hill inventory, 1971.

Terrace Hill Authority. Letter from Lawrence Ericsson, architect, December 13, 1977.

———. Report from Adrian Anderson, "Terrace Hill Management Plan," October 1, 1977.

———. "Terrace Hill Planning Series," 1978.

Terrace Hill Planning Commission. Pamphlet, Welcome to Terrace Hill, September 1972.

———. Report to the second session of the Sixty-fourth General Assembly, February 3, 1972.

United States District Court, District of Iowa. Journals, 1867-1892.

United States Supreme Court. Blennerhassett v. Sherman, 105 U.S. Reports 100; 1881.

———. Chicago, Milwaukee and Saint Paul Railway Co. v. Des Moines Union Railway Co., 254 U.S. Reports 196; 1920.

———. Cook County National Bank v. United States, 107 U.S. Reports 445; 1882.

Correspondence

Chicago Historical Society. Letter to authors about B.F. Allen, October 15, 1977.

General Services Administration, United States Government. Letters to authors about B.F. Allen, October 26, 1977, and January 24, 1978.

Skortman, Charles. Letter to authors about life at Terrace Hill, May 31, 1977.

Tometich, Frances. Letters to authors about life at Terrace Hill, June 2, 1977, January 17, 1978, and February 12, 1978.

Newsletters

Iowa Society for the Preservation of Historic Landmarks, 1975.
Polk County Historical Society, 1967-1975.

Speeches

Smith, Simpson P., to Mortgage Correspondents Association, Des Moines, May 3, 1967.

Miscellaneous

Commission on Chicago Historical and Architectural Landmarks. "Summary of Information on the Old Chicago Water Tower District," June 1971.

Hubbell trust. Inventory of major repairs, April 15, 1970.

Noun, Louise. Personal papers at Grinnell College, Grinnell, Iowa.

Telephone directory of Des Moines. Privately issued, 1881.

Terrace Hill Society. Report from Robert R. Harvey on early landscaping at Terrace Hill, June 22, 1977.

———. Pamphlet, "Your Invitation to the Terrace Hill Society."

Index

University of Michigan, 32
University Place (town of), 64
Usher, Earl, 95
Utah, 30, 37

V

Valley Limestone and Gravel Co., 71
Valley National Bank, 64
Van, Charley, 9
Vassar College, 26
Victoria Hotel, 64
Virginia, 8

W

Wabash Railroad Co., 61
Wabash, Saint Louis and Pacific Railroad, 48
Wachtmeister, Carl, 58
Wagner, William, 57, 77-78, 81, 83, 85-87, 95
Ward, John, 83, 85
Warren County, Iowa 10, 38
Washington D.C., 43, 58, 66
Washington, George, 25
Water Works Park, 80
Weaver, Anne, 71-72
Weaver, Jim, 66
Weaver, Philip, 72
West Des Moines High School, 71
West, Francis, 11, 22

West, Francis Mrs., 11, 31
West, William F., 43
Whitaker, George, 17
White House, 66, 81
White, Stephen, 12
Whitman, Henry L., 22
Whitney, Tom, 100
Wilcox, Jedidiah, 8
Wilde, Oscar, 16
Wilkins, Mary, 20
Williamson, William W., 22
Willits, Earl, 7, 92, 95, 99
Wilson, Woodrow, 66
Windsor, James, 78
Windsor, Mary Belle Hubbell (see Hubbell, Mary Belle)
Windsor, William, 91
Winkelman, William, 81
Wisconsin, 16, 73
Witmer, W.W., 81
Woodland Cemetery, 44, 70
Wright, George, 27
Wright, John, 25

Y

Yale University, 32, 71
YMCA, Des Moines, 71
Young, Madison, 10
YWCA, Des Moines, 71

Z

Ziegler, J. and Co., 25